Junior Youthbuilders

Also available from Marshall Pickering

Youthbuilders *Patrick Angier and Nick Aiken*
Big Ideas for Small Youth Groups *Patrick Angier and Nick Aiken*
Creative Ideas for Youth Evangelism *ed. Nick Aiken*

Junior Youthbuilders

• • •

A resource for reaching 11–14 year olds

PATRICK ANGIER

Illustrations by Ian Long

Marshall Pickering
An Imprint of HarperCollins*Publishers*

Marshall Pickering is an Imprint of
HarperCollins*Religious*
Part of HarperCollins*Publishers*
77–85 Fulham Palace Road, London W6 8JB

First published in Great Britain
in 1993 by Marshall Pickering

1 3 5 7 9 10 8 6 4 2

A catalogue record for this book is
available from the British Library

ISBN 0 551 02664-2

Typeset by Rowland Phototypesetting Limited
Bury St Edmunds, Suffolk
Printed and bound in Great Britain by
HarperCollinsManufacturing Glasgow

Contents

Acknowledgements

There are a number of people I would like to thank, all of whom are amazing and beautiful human beings! God delights in them, so they can endure a bit of praise from me.

First, thanks to Beverley, my wife, for the hours she has spent correcting the manuscript and making what I had written say what I really wanted to say!

Secondly, thanks to Neil Woodward for ideas, help and encouragement, as well as for five brilliant years of youth work together. He's got to be one of the best young Christian youth workers around.

Thirdly, I want to thank all those creative and imaginative people from whom I have borrowed ideas – in particular, thanks to Streetly Pathfinders for "Strawberry Tea", to Joe Cassey for "Advent Wall", to Jonathon Shaw for "Slime" and to all the youth teams at home and away over the years who have tried out these talks, games, activities and ideas.

Patrick Angier

An Exciting
or Awkward Age?

What's happening in the youth work world
What's happening in the young person's life
Getting off the roundabout
Making disciples
What is the world saying to young people?
Six issues to deal with
A different sort of problem: money
How to use this book

An Exciting or an Awkward Age?

Adolescence proves evolution...

It doesn't matter if your group is large or small, if it has been around since Noah or if it started last week. *Junior Youthbuilders* is for you: the person on the front line of Christian youth work with 11s to 14s. This is one of the most crucial ages for Christian discipleship. The seeds sown at this age can make the difference between young people leaving the Church or growing up to maturity in Christ.

Junior Youthbuilders is written to give you the resources to sow those seeds, with a mixture of teaching, fun and theory. The book contains numerous ideas for your youth programme and also shows you how to make those ideas work for you with your group.

WHAT'S HAPPENING IN THE YOUTH WORK WORLD

There are a number of changes happening in the youth scene.

Older youth groups are getting smaller

The needs of older young people and young adults have shown a change over recent years as the number of young people has declined by over 30 per cent in the last 15 years. There has been a departure from the desire to be in large groups. Smaller, more intimate groups are now common. These often compensate for the breakdown of family and societal caring units. This shift is being seen in changes in youth group size. Most of the statutory youth clubs operate with only a handful of young people on any one night. CYFA, the youth department of the Church Pastoral Aid Society, has said that the average youth group affiliated to them has under ten members, and figures for all other denominations are not too different.

Younger youth groups are growing

The situation with 11–14-year-olds is in the reverse. At this age, many young people enjoy being part of a larger group, and there are many thriving junior club nights and discos for this age. Pathfinders, the equivalent CPAS group, has an average affiliated size of 15 to 20 despite the falling population. Again, there are sociological reasons as well as spiritual ones behind this. It is important for us as Christian youth workers not to be afraid to take advantage of these trends. One of the reasons behind this book is to provide ideas and resources to facilitate a thriving work with 11–14-year-olds.

More youth work is being done by the voluntary sector

In a continued climate of cuts within the statutory youth work service, and the change of emphasis by many councils from supplying services to facilitating their provision, there is a growing role and a growing opportunity for church-based Christian youth work, and there are also the resources available for it. So make sure you find out the situation in your area and also what resources are available, e.g.:

Equipment grants
Running cost grants
County purchasing facility

Minibus loans
Workshops and community arts groups
Subsidized leisure facilities
Training
Equipment hire and loan

Each area is different, so find out what is available.

There is greater competition for young people's time

Whatever we do, it has to be of a high quality as well as godly. Young people have the choice to attend or not to, and the range of options open to them is getting progressively larger. Traditional uniformed organizations, sports clubs and music lessons are now supplemented by martial arts, TV and video, video games, outdoor pursuits and the ever-increasing pressure of school-work at all ages.

WHAT'S HAPPENING IN THE YOUNG PERSON'S LIFE

External changes

School

This is the age when young people move to Secondary School: they go from being the eldest to all of a sudden being the youngest. Sometimes this move involves leaving friends and having to develop new friends in a strange environment. Often the young people can go through a time of being shy and unconfident, while some may experience bullying.

Organizations

At this age members move up from the security of Cubs and Brownies to Scouts and Guides. As with the change of schools, this will mean suddenly being the youngest again, a strange environment and for some, humiliating rituals.

Church

The local church is often uncertain how to handle 11–14s, as they are too old for Junior Church and yet still a bit young for the Youth Group. Parents may want their youngsters still to be children, and yet the youngsters themselves want more independence. Groups like Pathfinders and Scripture Union's Lasers do an excellent job of bridging the gap, but many churches have nothing to offer this age and, sadly, the young people are often left feeling that they do not belong. A feeling of belonging fostered amongst kids of this age can be really positive, leading to the forming of lasting relationships.

Society

Society's expectations of young people change at this age. They can be charged with an offence; see a "12" film unaccompanied; be employed on a part-time basis; be sent to a detention centre and enter a pub whilst accompanied by an adult. Society begins to attribute responsibility and accountability as well as giving opportunities.

Family

It may be at this age that a young person has his/her first experience of bereavement, with the loss of a grandparent or other relative: this adds to the unease created by all the changes they are experiencing.

Internal changes

Physical development

Height

This age range contains both the minimum height gain per year and also the maximum. What an added complication to the already confused teenager! His/her uncertainty about his/her development is accentuated by the fact that others may or may not be experiencing the same growth rate. Being too tall can be just as awful as being too small. This time of rapid growth may result in a lack of co-ordination and clumsiness, especially for boys, as the brain may think the body is smaller than it now is. Girls often begin their growth spurt at 11 or 12, boys more often at 12 or 13. Growth may happen at a steady rate, with less confusion, or it may happen all at once.

Body

The growth in height is accompanied by bone strengthening and muscle toning, a process which will continue into young adulthood.

Voice

For boys this is the age when their voices break, and this often causes a lot of embarrassment.

Sexual development

For both boys and girls puberty can be a distressing time. Girls experience breast development, the growth of body hair and

the beginning of periods. Boys experience genital development, the appearance of body hair and the added embarrassment of a breaking voice.

The way in which young people react to these changes
varies. I know of one lad who stood naked in front of the
largest mirror in the house and called to his family to come
and see, because he had his first pubic hair! Another lad went
around wearing a sanitary towel because he expected his
period to start. I know of two schools where the boys were
upset that they were going to have periods, because the girls
had had sex education lessons and had then reported the
information to the lads!

For girls, being the first to be seen wearing a bra in PE can
be either the height of embarrassment or an opportunity to
boast and be held in high regard. For others, having to cope
with the unpredictability and pain of their period can be a real
trial.

These are some of the changes experienced by our young
people at this age.

Internal pressures

Physical

Sexual development can create feelings of inadequacy; boys
can feel guilty about having wet dreams; girls can have
crushes. This is the age not only of the Pop Hero but also of
the Youth Leader Idol and the Teacher Hero. Yes, you too
can be the victim of a crush! One girl would collect anything
at all to do with the teacher she had a crush on. Sometimes
these crushes can be obsessive, but mostly they are just
normal.

Independence

Young people need space to grow and develop – they need room to try things out (and get it wrong!). If parental control is enforced too far, rebellion will result. But if not enough guidelines are given the young person will lack direction and values and may be overwhelmed by his/her new freedom.

Moods

The internal changes going on in young people often produce massive mood changes. These are unpredictable, and the young person can go from being on top of the world to being in the depths of despair, and this can happen within hours or even minutes. As a result he/she may find it difficult to put things in perspective and to cope with growing respon-sibilities.

External pressures

The boss of MTV once said, "We don't influence young people, we own them." TV, videos, magazines, ads . . . all of these put immense pressures on our young people. "Unless you look like this you are not *in*," young people are told. "Unless you listen to this band you are not an OK person." The messages are not always explicit ones, but they are received loud and clear. No young person lives up to the media stereotype they think they have to be; all will experi-ence some feelings of inadequacy and will develop strategies to cope with these. I could write a whole book on the teen-media problem, but a much better idea would be for you to buy some of the magazines which young people read and to record some of the programmes they watch. Look at what they are saying and how they say it. How many "ugly people" are ever included in features or covers? What does the magazine/programme say about self-image? How is the image in the magazine/programme linked to the products which are being advertised?

HOW TO APPLY ALL OF THIS TO YOUR YOUTH GROUP

1. *Create a welcoming atmosphere.* A youth group session starts when the first young person arrives and finishes when the last young person leaves. We need to set an example by making people feel welcome and included. Here are five ways to make the young people feel welcome:

1 Know their names – even if it means making a special effort to remember them.
2 Have the room ready when they arrive so that you are not too busy to listen.
3 Don't "grill" them but talk and share with them.
4 Try not to embarrass them (e.g. "Hello everyone, this is Jane, she's new this week. Stand on that chair, Jane, and tell us what the Lord has done in your life!").
5 Make sure the group welcomes new people.

One of the problems which nearly every youth worker faces is that of finding the right place to meet – a place where a wecloming atmosphere can be created. The choice is often between the cold church hall or someone's house. But it is possible to be creative with where we meet as well as with what we teach. For example, in our youth group we once taught about discipleship as we walked round a local lake, stopping and using different things as object lessons as we found them. (The session had a really good feel to it and many young people saw parallels with the Bible passages that we looked at.) The situations can be varied: you could teach about the character of God on a hill-top, about Peter or Paul in prison from a police cell, or about being rescued by Jesus at the local fire station.

2. *Help the young people to feel included by giving them responsibilities* that challenge them and make use of their gifts and abilities. Always encourage them when they are successful, and don't be unhelpfully critical when things go wrong. The young people will inevitably make some mistakes.

3. *When playing games, be aware of the size and ability differences in the group.* Choose games that are co-operative or where the size factor is not so important. Our lads went through a phase of wanting to play American Football as a means of bullying the smaller lads. You need to be aware of these kinds of things when planning your programme.

4. *If young people are embarrassed or upset in any situation it is our responsibility to rescue them and to protect their dignity before our own.* We should never use "put-downs" or force people to participate against their will. Of course, some young people need encouragement to help them to join in, but that's something quite different.

5. *This age is activity-orientated:* they enjoy doing things and being active, as they have a low boredom threshold. When they reach the age of about 14 they stop being so activity-orientated, and are then much more into sitting around chatting. We need to bear this in mind when planning programmes etc.

GETTING OFF THE ROUNDABOUT

One of the dangers in youth work is that of the programme becoming and end in itself rather than a means of helping young people to be disciples of Jesus. This can result in the "roundabout phenomenon" in which the summer beach barbecue is followed by the autumn weekend away is followed by the Christmas party is followed by . . . The programme follows the same pattern each year. Things are done because they have always been done, and the measure of success is how the numbers compare with the year before. The problem with the roundabout is that it moves too fast: things can appear to be going well, but the programme ends up going nowhere.

An alternative approach to programming would be to ask ourselves the questions below:

1. How does this activity contribute towards the overall aim of our youth work?
2. Who are we aiming this programme at? Are we trying to draw in new people, are we aiming at the core members? etc.
3. Why is it important to teach/organize this particular session/event now?
4. What alternative ways could we use to achieve the same objectives, and are they preferable to this?
5. When did we last do a programme like this, and were there lessons we should take into account from then?

This approach of questioning our programme against the objectives for the group ensures that we are far more likely to achieve the results we want and that everyone knows where they are headed. It also leaves nobody in any doubt as to why the youth work is being undertaken. We have all heard of churches that organize monthly discos, and the leaders wonder why they never see the same young people in church on a Sunday morning . . .

The most important thing by far, however, is to have a clearly defined *aim* for your youth work that all the leaders share.

Exercise

1. On a piece of paper write in 20 words or less the aim of the youth work you are involved in.
2. Write down three ways in which the youth work tries to meet the aim.
3. If you are part of a team, do this as a group exercise and share the answers. You may be quite surprised with the diversity of answers that the group comes up with. They may include things like:
   * to help the young people reach their full potential
   * to provide a meeting-place
   * to win young people for Christ
   * to interest young people in the church.

MAKING DISCIPLES

Once we have got off the roundabout, we can begin to look at how to use our youth group programme to aid us in discipling young people. You must, as a youth leader, be very familiar with this principle: "What young people hear, they forget, but what they do, they remember." How can we produce a programme to overcome this problem? It is a great start to have integrated programming, where everything in the evening connects with the theme and where the games, activities, teaching etc. are mixed together. This is also helpful because attention-spans at this age are short. The second way to use this to our advantage is to provide opportunities for action. There is no reason why 11–14s should not be involved in any of the activities below. Go through the list and tick where appropriate, to gain an overview of your group's activities.

Activity	They already do it	They could do it	Not sure if they should do it
Praying			
Bible study			
Helping with creche			
Helping with Sunday School			
Read in church			
Digging of garden			
Holy Spirit ministry			
Church cleaning team			
Singing in music group			
Playing instrument			
Drama or dance group			
Greeting people			
Making coffee			
Poster design			
Banner making			
Visiting elderly			
Babysitting for free			
Giving out books			
Serving			
Leaflet distribution			
Hospital visits			

The young people's involvement in these ministries benefits both the church and the youth group, and it also benefits the young people themselves in a number of ways:

1. They will not see church and Christianity as childish. All too often we treat young people, who are making important decisions about life, values and education, as "passive consumers". It is very rare to lose a young person from a youth group because it is over-challenging. It is far more likely that they will be lost through boredom and under-stimulation, and they decide that Christianity is only for children as a result.

2. Learning to minister and being discipled cannot be separated from ministering and discipling. Jesus demonstrated to the twelve disciples, taught them and then sent them out to do likewise. He then reviewed the situation and sent them out again with 60 others to do the same. We must be constantly encouraging, demonstrating and sending out our young people to minister at a level appropriate to them right from their earliest days. The benefit to the young people is that they will develop a confident and articulate faith.

3. The young people will make a greater impact on their non-Christian friends at school because they are involved and more likely to be visible in the community.

WHAT IS THE WORLD SAYING TO YOUNG PEOPLE?

The world of the young person today is not as friendly a place as it was 20 or 30 years ago. There are a number of reasons for this, but we need only be concerned with the dominant world values that today's young people have to face.

The six big lies

1 YOU ARE WHAT YOU LOOK LIKE.
2 YOU ARE WHAT YOU ACCOMPLISH.
3 YOU ARE WHAT YOU WATCH.
4 YOU ARE WHAT YOU CONSUME.
5 YOU ARE WHAT YOU WANT.
6 YOU ARE ALONE.

The world lies to young people and all too often they accept this without challenging it. The Kingdom of God has a rather different set of values to those of the world. We must begin to recognize this and challenge the worldly values in our own lives by asking:

1. What are the priorities in our lives? Where these are based on worldly values, the young people will pick this up.

2. Who do you and your fellow leaders spend your time with? Is it the successful, outgoing and confident young people, those who do well in most situations? Or do we love the outcast, the lonely . . . those whom the world is not so keen on?

3. Which young people get invited into leadership positions? Those most able, those who are most popular, those who want to or those who will do the job best?

4. When you use teams, how are they chosen? Is someone left to last and made to feel less able? Do we compound that young person's feelings of failure by saying by our actions that God thinks they're a failure too?

5. Have a programme that discourages the young people from treating the evening as a mere fashion parade.

The six truths

Here are six truths which we need to emphasize to our young people:

1. You are beautiful to God. The world might measure by outward appearance, but the kingdom of God is concerned for those whom the world rejects. Whenever Jesus met anyone, He only saw the beauty of a child of God created in the image of the Father, whatever the world said to them about their appearance. We should mirror Jesus' attitude in our treatment of our young people.

2. God values *you* more highly than any of your achievements. What you *are* and not what you *do* is what is most important to your Heavenly Father.

3. God is our Creator. He knows our inmost thoughts; He knows what makes us tick. Our identity is found in this intimate relationship with our Creator, not in obeying the dictates of TV or advertising.

4. Having the right material things will not make you happy. Happiness is found in a relationship with God. If happiness is to be found in material possessions, why is it that those with so much are still unsatisfied and those with so little are often happier?

5. God is not some divine Father Christmas distributing blessings. He calls us to deny ourselves, take up our cross and follow Him. In doing so we discover true happiness. Our youth work needs to reflect the cost of commitment to Christ.

6. You are not alone. There is a God in Heaven who loves you enough to die for you, and one day you will meet Him as your Judge. You are not the chance product of a meaningless universe – you have purpose and meaning. As leaders we need to help the young people to recognize this in ways they can understand.

SIX ISSUES TO DEAL WITH

Sex

"Oh no! Not sex and relationships! We have enough of that, and everyone's fed up with having safe sex talks at school. So why do we need to cover it at the youth group?"

1. Because the foundations need to be laid at an early age. Young people need to have a biblical understanding of relationships, and by the time they are 14 it is often too late.

2. Because the world is already bombarding them through TV, magazines etc. with unbiblical teaching. We need to teach young people to challenge the accepted norms of society and to hold fast to their Christian teaching.

3. They live in a world that lacks absolutes. Clear teaching gives them a standpoint from which to judge and value things.

4. Pregnancy, abortion and sexually transmitted diseases are on the increase in this age range. The statistics for Christian youth groups are better than those for society at large, but they will only stay so if we give our young people clear teaching.

5. God wants young people to enjoy being young, to have fun doing things together and being part of a group and to learn intimacy in special friendships without feeling that they have to prove themselves sexually.

6. Young people need to discover their sexuality (i.e. their maleness or femaleness) and how good it is to be created in the image of God. This discovery can be damaged by the guilt and hurts of failed sexual relationships.

Alcohol

Adolescent young people want to take on adult behaviour patterns. One of the few rites of passage in our culture is the legitimization of alcohol at the age of 18. Many adults attach a lot of importance to alcohol, so it is no wonder that many young people and even children use alcohol in illegal and self-destructive ways.

What should our attitude as youth leaders be, and how can we teach constructively without reducing the Gospel of grace to a Pharisaic list of do's and don'ts? As youth leaders we need to show that it's possible to have a good time without alcohol – indeed, a better time. Our youth group social events need to develop positive role-models of what having fun is about, so that the young people have a real alternative. We also need to give young people responsibility. If they are looking for rights of passage into the adult world, then to treat them as children is to drive them to do exactly what we don't want them to do.

Drugs

Today drug-taking is an everyday occurrence for many young people in all sorts of areas. We know of youngsters as young as nine who have been offered drugs at school, and yet other young people will go through the whole of school life without ever seeing any. Drugs are not the product or province of any social class: they seem just as prevalent in the wealthy private schools as in the UPA comprehensives. How do we prepare without encouraging, warn without scaring? How do we ensure that Christian young people have the knowledge and preparation to deal with situations when they occur?

With all these issues, it's good to think through the options and responses, so that when such a situation occurs you have some guiding principles and information to enable you to deal with it.

Parents

Almost all the young people in your youth group will have to cope with these (and, very often, so will you!). If it's hard for the young people to grow up, it's even harder for many parents to come to terms with the challenges which their teenagers present during this transition period between childhood and adulthood. It is a time of conflict and frequent mood swings. As a youth leader, it is all too easy to be caught in the middle of conflicts quite by accident: "The youth leader says I have to be at music group this evening, so you can't ground me! . . ." "I never received the letter saying they would be back late . . ."

Ten tips to keep parents sane

1. Always give dates, times and costs in advance of any activity.

2. Ensure that all correspondence reaches its destination, even if this means posting it.

3. Stick to schedules and arrangements. Always try to be back when you say you will be. If you are delayed, let parents know.

4. If you are going to a late event, offer to take the young people home afterwards.

5. Keep an attendance register (this can double up as a subs book), so that if the need ever arises, parents can check if their youngster is actually turning up or if instead he/she is bunking off somewhere.

6. Never let young people out without knowing where they are going and why.

7. Try to meet with the parents of new members (especially those from non-church backgrounds) as soon as possible, so that they can be assured that you are not a three-headed brain-washing alien and so that you can begin to evangelize them!

8. Invite them along to one of your evening meetings to see what happens. They may even come!

9. Hold regular parents' evenings, where they can meet the leaders, see what has been happening in the programme and look at the houseparty photos of their youngster buried in instant whip etc.

10. Always treat the parents with respect, and remember that God values them, even if their youngsters don't.

Peers

Surveys have consistently shown that the most important people to young people in their decision-making are other young people. As youth leaders we need to question this on the one hand and use it to our advantage on the other. Why the statistics don't seem to ring true:

1. Young people look for adult affirmation: they can do anything with praise and encouragement.

2. The all-important peer group is often negative, critical and exclusive, leaving young people left out but trying and wanting to fit in.

3. Young people want to be grown up, so they are looking to adult role models, even if they never verbalize it as such.

What does this mean for youth leadership?

1. We need to provide positive adult role models.

2. We need to create a group that is inclusive and welcoming, where strangers can feel at home and where those who all to often are left out are valued and given worth.

3. A group where encouragement is the order of the day and where leaders don't score cheap points by knocking young people.

4. A group that provides positive alternatives to destructive lifestyles and values.

5. We, as leaders, set the tone by being honest about ourselves, owning up when we make mistakes, giving credit to those who deserve it when something goes well etc.

Abuse

This issue is one of the hardest to handle, especially if you have a young person whose father is a deacon or churchwarden or even the vicar or pastor, and they are being abused in some way at home. Whatever you do, tread carefully.

1. Always seek help from specialists such as the social services, the NSPCC, Childline etc. Also talk confidentially to church leaders. Don't try to go it alone, but take advice.

2. Believe the young person. If they trust you enough to tell you, then it is the least you can do to reciprocate that trust. It may be that they are lying, and we should weigh the evidence. But if a young person has taken the huge personal risk of telling us his/her hurts and experiences, then we must believe them. This might be their only chance, or you might be the only person they can tell, and how you respond will affect their healing and recovery. Of course, we should not take rash

action, and, as we said above, it is vital to seek advice, but at the end of the day, if they are lying, so what? We may end up looking foolish, but our pride isn't the most important thing.

3. Be concerned for the young person: support them with your prayers and, if appropriate, with your time and counsel. You may need to be a place of refuge, but this can get you into deep water, as you are dealing with minors, so again seek advice.

4. Don't break the confidence. Gossip in the church will not help the young person or the parents. One difficult question is whether or not to tell your pastor. You are under his God-given authority, but you are also in the young person's trust. If you break that trust, it might make the young person's situation much worse.

You're probably at this point saying that you don't have any abused young people in your youth group. But my experience is that there are abused young people in many youth groups.

What is abuse? The NSPCC defines child abuse in four main ways:

1. *Physical abuse*
Where parents hurt, injure or even kill a young person.

2. *Sexual abuse*
Where parents use a young person for their own sexual gratification.

3. *Neglect*
Where parents fail to meet the young person's basic needs for food, clothes, warmth and medical care.

4. *Emotional abuse*
Where constant lack of love and affection or threats, verbal attacks, taunting and shouting destroy a young person's confidence and self-esteem, so that they become nervous and withdrawn.

A DIFFERENT SORT OF PROBLEM: MONEY

I have yet to meet the church treasurer who comes up to you on the first day of the youth group's financial year and says, "Spend whatever you need – don't worry about it!"

Many of you reading this will have no youth budget from your church, and you have to pay for most things yourself. You've tried all the legitimate ways to have a youth budget (e.g. writing to the church council, talking to the pastor, forming a youth support group to argue for you etc.), and you don't want to use a more direct route (e.g. kidnap the vicar/ minister and say they can't have him back till you get some money!), so what do you do?

An alternative form of funding is needed. These are the main ways in which my youth work has obtained finances:

county council grant aid
trust funds
private gifts from church members
members' subs
fund-raising events
tuck shop/coffee bar sales
revenue from events/trips etc.

These are all plusses on the income side. On the expenditure side, we need to balance our expensive activities with less expensive ones to ensure that finances don't become a problem. For example, don't do too many food activities.

HOW TO USE THIS BOOK

Be inventive: adapt and change ideas to fit your situation. Just because things worked one way for one group doesn't mean they can't work a different way with your group.

Have fun discipling your young people. It is important, but it is not so serious that it can't be enjoyable. Jesus was accused of being a glutton and a drunkard by the Pharisees. Obviously, we're not recommending either option, but there is nothing wrong with young people coming away from an evening having had a really good time, as well as having discovered/experienced/done something towards the group's *aim*.

Don't let your youth work replace the time you spend on your personal devotional life. Reading books full of youth group ideas is great and can really encourage us and challenge us, but our youth ministry will only have the power it needs to have if we have a close and real relationship with God, and we can only have a relationship like that if we make our devotional life our top priority.

2

Teaching Sessions

Exploding for Jesus
Just Good Friends
Option Plays & Tension Getters
Construct a Christian
The Option Choice
Monopoly
Dressed Not to Kill
Firm Foundations
The Gift Auction
24-Hour Dilemma

TEACHING

Albert taught his youth group by example.

Exploding for Jesus

Aim

To look, in a fun way, at the types of transformation that Jesus can bring in to our lives.

Equipment

Uncooked popcorn, salt, oil, a large saucepan with a top, honey.

Venue

This session is especially good for a small youth group meeting in a home or in a church hall.

Warm-up

Play some explosive ice-breakers.

Main session

1. Organize the group into three teams (or if yours is a small group, do everything together). Their task is to produce three different sorts of popcorn.

Team 1: Your task is to produce a bowl of scrumptious, hot, plain popcorn.

Team 2: Your task is to produce a bowl of sizzling, salty popcorn.

Team 3: Your task is to produce a bowl of mouth-watering, sweet, syrup-coated popcorn.

2. After the teams have completed their tasks, and before all the popcorn is eaten (this isn't easy!), gather the group back together and do some popcorn tasting. Give each team's popcorn a mark out of ten. The winning team then makes some more at the end of the evening for everyone to share.

3. Digging into the Bible.

Team 1: Read Matthew 5:13. What is the salt of the earth? Can you explain in your own words how we can be the salt of the earth? Read Acts 8:26–40. What does this passage show us about being salt?

Team 2: Read Exodus 3:8. What does the writer mean when he talks of a land flowing with milk and honey? Can you explain in your own words how we can be like milk and honey? Read Mark 3:7–12. Why was it that people were attracted to Jesus?

Team 3: Read Acts 3:19; Matthew 4:17; Acts 13:47. What do these passages tell us about being changed when we encounter Jesus? How are people changed by Jesus today?

If possible put a leader with each team, or move between teams to help where necessary.

When the teams have finished, ask a spokesperson from each to report back to everyone. If they have any questions, answer them now.

Talk

Give a short talk including the following points:

1. We need to be exploded for Jesus – i.e. we need to be totally transformed; the old self needs to be blown away. Our hard outer shells have to go. We need to be put into a transforming environment. The process changes us, and afterwards we are no longer the same as those who have not been through it. Noisy conversion is not easy, but it is dynamic. (You can use

what happens to popcorn when it is cooked as an analogy of what happens when a young person is converted.)

2. Have you exploded for Jesus? Have you asked the Holy Spirit into your life so that He can change you? Do people notice that you are different?

3. Close with a time of prayer, and then give people an opportunity to explode!

Just good friends

Aim

To teach the group members to apply Christian values to their friendships.

Preparation

Prepare six full-size paper human shapes. Label them "Friend 1", "Friend 2" and so on, and stick them up on the wall at the start of the session.

Warm-up

Play Hug Tag for about ten minutes. In this game, one person is "It". He/she has to tag everyone. When a person is tagged they are out. If they are hugging someone they cannot be tagged. Hugs must be face-to-face, with arms round each other. No hug can last more than five seconds. You cannot hug the same person twice. The last person to be tagged is "It" in the next game.

If some people never get hugged, and others get everyone wanting to hug them, don't worry, as this will help with the teaching session.

Main session

1. Give a copy of the friendship questionnaire to each person and ask them to fill it in.

FRIENDSHIP QUESTIONNAIRE

1 Do you have any friends? ....

How many? .... Be honest ....

2 How many of your friends have larger feet than you and how many have smaller feet?

Larger .... Smaller ....

3 How many enemies do you have? ....

Are they larger than you? Yes/No ....

4 Write the name of your best friend backwards ......

5 Do you tell your best friend secrets that you don't tell anybody else? ....

List three .... Only joking!

Why do you tell your best friend secrets? ....

....

6 Has your best friend ever told other people your secrets? ....

How did you feel? ....

7 Do you and your best friend ever:

argue? ....

fight? ....

share milkshakes? ....

pray together? ....

8 If you didn't have any friends, what would you do at the weekends? ....

9 How many friends is it good to go around in a group with? ....

10 How would you describe what a friend is? ....

....

....

This sheet will be collected in

Collect in the sheets and ask people to share their answers to question 10 and any comments they might wish to make.

2. Give an A4 sheet of paper to each person and ask them to tear it neatly into four pieces. Ask them to write on each piece one characteristic of a good friend. When they have done that they are to fold the pieces of paper up and put them in the bucket in the middle. Leaders also need to do this, but they should write characteristics that people don't often associate with best friends, e.g. blind, smelly, poor, spotty, lonely, bad at sport, fat, orphan, unfashionable . . . Think of ones appropriate to your group.

3. When everyone has their papers in the bucket ask a volunteer to come out and choose six papers and to read them out and go and stick them on Friend 1. While he/she is sticking them on, ask for another volunteer to do the same to Friend 2. When all six Friends have their characteristics on them, ask the group to read them all.

4. Ask everyone to stand by the Friend they would most like to be friends with. There should now be a group beside each Friend. The people in each group now share briefly why they chose that particular Friend. If possible put a leader with each group.

Bible investigation

The world often tells us what people should be like and who we should be friends with, but let's see what God's Word has to say about friendship.

Group 1: Paul & Barnabas. Read Acts 9:26–30; 11:22–26; 13:1–3.

Group 2: David & Jonathan. Read 1 Samuel 18:1–4; 19:1–7; 20:1–4.

Group 3: Jesus & Peter. Read John 21:15–19; Mark 14:27–31.

Group 4: Ruth & Naomi. Read Ruth 1:1–22.

Group 5: Jacob & Rachel. Read Genesis 29:10–30.

Group 6: Paul & Onesimus. Read all of Philemon!

When the groups have completed their Bible studies ask them to report back to the whole group. Then round off and close in prayer.

Option plays and tension getters

These are useful for teaching on any topic or situation, especially issues in the local and/or national news. Option plays get the young people to think in terms of the consequences of their actions, and tension getters teach them to defend their actions.

Option plays

An option play is where you present a situation to the youth group, e.g.:

1. You are invited by some friends to go shoplifting in the lunch break.
2. Your mum is seeing another man and has told you not to tell your father.
3. You and your friends are caught smoking at school.
4. You have arranged to go out with a boy/girl but another boy/girl you really fancy asks you to go somewhere.

Divide the young people into groups of four or five and give each group a different situation. They list all their options in that situation, and then they write down three consequences for each course of action. Finally all the groups report back and discuss their findings.

Tension getters

Describe a situation (e.g. a story from a newspaper). Divide the young people into two groups. One group has to defend one view of the situation, while the other group defends the opposite view. Let them argue out the rights and wrongs of the issue.

Construct a Christian

Aim

To look at the young people's stereotypes of what a Christian is and to challenge these where necessary.

Equipment

Wallpaper, paint, charcoal, scissors, chairs, tables, a bag of sweets, paper and pencils for everyone.

Preparation

Make enough instruction cards so that each young person has one. Fill them in with a variety of ages and names, and using both sexes.

INSTRUCTION CARD

Your Christian is called ....
Aged .... Sex ....

Draw a human outline. Cut it out and paint it according to how you see this person as a Christian – e.g. what would they wear? Would they be trendy? etc.

Warm-up

Ask for six volunteers to come out to the front to be your panel of experts. Sit them on the chairs in two rows of three, behind the tables. Two contestants taken from the rest of the group come out to the front to attempt to win a packet of sweets. The game is played as follows:

1. Give each contestant in turn a word.
2. The contestant and the panel members write down on the paper provided the first thing that the given word brings to mind.
3. The contestant and then the panel share what they wrote.
4. The contestant scores one point for each member of the panel who has written the same answer as he/she has.
5. Play two rounds. The winner is the contestant with the most points.

Main session

1. Divide the group into teams of four.
2. Talk to the group along these lines: "We all have stereotypical views of what summer holidays, old houses, school dinners etc. are like. What are our stereotypical images of what a Christian is like? What I want you to do is to construct a stereotypical Christian from the information given you on your instruction card."
3. After the teams have had enough time to do this, get them all to introduce their Christian to the rest of the group and to talk about what they are like and why.
4. Hold a vote with the whole group as to which of the stereotypes/characters was the most probable. Then look at John 1:12 and talk about what a Christian is really like – i.e. someone who has received Jesus as his/her Lord and Saviour and who is a child of God.

5. End with prayer, and provide an opportunity for the young people to chat about being a Christian. They might also want to talk about their fears of becoming like their stereotypes.

The option choice

Aim

To help the young people to discover where they stand on moral issues, to get them used to articulating their Christian faith and to challenge the view that there is no right and wrong.

Warm-up

Play a selection of ice-breakers that involve moving around teams and pairs, e.g. Clumping (see *Youthbuilders*), Body Dice (ditto), Colour Clash (see Chapter 7 of this book) and Human Dominoes (ditto).

Main session

Prepare a list of alternatives like those below. Yell them out, pointing one option to one end of the hall and the other option to the other end of the hall. E.g.:

rich/poor (rich = top end, poor = bottom end)
famous/unknown
fat/thin
male/female
short/tall
Christian/non-Christian
black/white
married/single

Call out each option in turn. The young people have to decide which of the options they would rather be and then go to the appropriate end of the hall.

When they have all decided and moved (no one is allowed to sit on the fence), ask for volunteers to explain their choice. (Or pick on individuals who seem only to have moved with their friends.) Allow people on either side to challenge individuals' positions or to try and persuade people to move.

Hints

This activity is a helpful transition from a games session to a teaching/discussion session. E.g. pair up a couple from either end to talk to the rest of the group about their choice on any one topic.

This is also a good activity for joint youth group events. It can help the young people to discover what they have in common as well as where their differences lie.

Monopoly

Aim

To teach the young people about fairness, in a fun way.

Equipment

One Monopoly set for every six players, a video machine, a TV, a Tearfund video or something similar.

Preparation

Place the following amounts of money into labelled envelopes (you will need one set of envelopes for each group of six players):

Player 1:   5x£500,   1x£100, 1x£50, 1x£20, 2x£10, 1x£5, 0x£1
Player 2:   3x£500,   1x£100, 1x£50, 1x£20, 2x£10, 1x£5, 2x£1
Player 3:   1x£500,   5x£100, 1x£50, 1x£20, 1x£10, 1x£5, 1x£1
Player 4:   0x£500,   3x£100, 2x£50, 1x£20, 1x£10, 1x£5, 3x£1
Player 5:   0x£500,   0x£100, 2x£50, 2x£20, 2x£10, 2x£5, 3x£1
Player 6:   0x£500,   0x£100, 0x£50, 0x£20, 0x£10, 0x£5, 12x£1

Action

1. Divide the young people into groups of six. Distribute a set of envelopes among each group – do it randomly, so that there can be no accusations of favouritism.
2. Ask everyone to play the game for half an hour, and the player with the most assets and money at the end of the time is the winner.
3. As they open their envelopes to get the money out there may be some mutterings that you have got it wrong. Say as little as possible, but explain that what they have is what they are to play with.
4. When half an hour is up, ask everyone to count up their money and assets and to write the total down (property is worth the purchase price).
5. Gather all the groups back together. Record how much money each player had at the end, and declare an overall winner. Discuss the game – who made the most, who lost the most etc.
6. Ask the group to go to one end of the room if they thought the game was fair and the other end if they thought it wasn't fair. Let them challenge the other side as to why it was or wasn't fair. When the debate dies down ask if they can think of any situations in life that remind them of the unfairness of the game. Encourage them to say why the situations they mention are like the game.
7. Finish with a video by Tear Fund or a similar organization. The video should talk about some of the issues in the developing world, and how young people can take action to

help. Close by challenging the young people to take some action.

Dressed not to kill!

Aim

To look at our values and priorities in how we dress, and to evaluate these in the light of Scripture.

Equipment

£8 in cash per team, lots of newspapers, a flipchart, pens, pencils, sellotape.

Preparation

This activity takes place over two weeks, so read it through carefully before planning which bits to do on which week.

Week 1
Warm-up

Play a game called Fashion Design, described below:
1. Divide the group into pairs. If there is an odd number get a leader to take part.
2. Give each pair a pile of newspapers and a reel of sellotape.
3. The task is to dress one partner up in the newspapers. The best fashion design will be judged on style, artistic flair, originality etc.
4. After twenty minutes ask the models to line up, and the leaders choose the winner or winners.
5. Have a two-minute war with all the newspapers, or play snowball fights with them.

6. Put the newspapers into sacks and take them to the recycling centre.

Main session

1. Hand out to everyone a "What's your trend?" rating sheet and ask them to fill it in.

What's your trend?

(a) *You are invited to the school square's birthday tea. Do you:*
  (i) Turn up in your best Sunday clothes and hope no one sees?
  (ii) Turn up in your street clothes and not be allowed in by the parents?
  (iii) Say you are away that day?
  (iv) Emigrate?

(b) *You have to take your younger brother shopping for a school shirt. Do you:*
  (i) Go out at 9 a.m. sharp to avoid seeing any of your friends?
  (ii) Drag all your friends along too so that they can offer their help and advice?
  (iii) Buy a totally unsuitable shirt so that you will never be asked to do it again?
  (iv) Have a great time shopping with little brother and do loads of window shopping together?

(c) *Your mother is taking you and some friends out for the day, and she comes down dressed in a yellow outfit with pink and orange spots. Do you:*
  (i) Fall ill rapidly and lie on the floor, frothing at the mouth?
  (ii) Tell her that the outfit doesn't match yours and suggest that she wears something else?
  (iii) Tell all your friends that she's going on to a fancy dress party later and hasn't time to change?

    (iv) Rush upstairs and put on your matching outfit and stun all your friends?

(d) *For your birthday you are given some money to spend on clothes. Do you:*
    (i) Put it in the bank until you need it?
    (ii) Buy one item that costs all you have?
    (iii) Go round all the markets and charity shops looking for bargains?
    (iv) Buy as many street cred items as you can and pose at every opportunity?

(e) *Which of the following is the most important for you?*
    (i) Having the latest album by your favourite band.
    (ii) Having the latest *Young People's Every Day with Jesus* booklet.
    (iii) Having the latest training shoes.
    (iv) Having the latest designer jeans.

(f) *When a totally "in" schoolfriend sees you dressed in casual clothes, do you:*
    (i) Worry about what they think and try not to be seen?
    (ii) Dash over the road to say "Hi!" and to comment on their outfit?
    (iii) Study what they are wearing and ensure that next time you shop for clothes, that's what you get?
    (iv) Go home to your parents and complain that they never buy you trendy clothes?

(g) *You go somewhere and are very inappropriately dressed. Do you:*
    (i) Panic?
    (ii) Pretend that you are someone else?
    (iii) Find a quiet corner and hide?
    (iv) Carry on regardless and have a great time?

(h) *One morning you are so sleepy that you go to school in your pyjamas. What do you do?* ....
....
....

2. When everyone has completed the sheet label the four corners of the room (i), (ii), (iii) and (iv) to correspond to the four answers to each question on the sheet. Read out the first question and ask people to go to the corner that corresponds to their answer. Do the same for the rest of the questions. (Some young people will find this difficult if they are the only one in a corner.) Let the group challenge, question or comment on any of the solutions.

3. When you have gone through all the questions ask people to choose a corner according to the criteria below:

(i)   "I'm a complete fashion slave. If it's not trendy it's not good enough."
(ii) "I'm a complete fashion rebel. If it's in, I don't wear it."
(iii) "I'm a parent clone. If Mum and Dad wear it, that's what I like to wear."
(iv) "I'm a comfort critter. If it feels comfortable, who cares if it's in or not?"

4. These corner groups are now the teams for the next exercise. If you have a particularly large or small group you may have to make some adjustments, but you need to finish with teams of between four and six with similar fashion sense. You may want boys and girls to be in separate teams.

5. Give each team an envelope containing their fashion challenge and £8 in cash.

Fashion challenge

(a) Your task is to dress one member of your team using the money provided.
(b) You are not allowed to use any of her/his own clothes, apart from underwear.
(c) You will have to present your outfit at next week's meeting and talk about the items you have chosen.

Week 2
Main session

1. Set up the meeting-place as best you can for a fashion show. Mark out an area for the catwalk. Use spotlights, music, etc.
2. When the members arrive give them time to dress their models, and then get everyone to sit round the catwalk. Ask each team in turn to display their model and to talk about where they went, what they bought, how they adapted things etc.
3. After the teams have made their presentations give them a cheer and announce a winner, if you have judges.
4. Then brainstorm onto the flipchart, asking these questions:

What makes an item fashionable?
What makes an item unfashionable?

When there is a good long list and everyone who wants to say something has had the opportunity to do so, ask everyone to return to their teams.
5. Ask the teams to discuss these questions:
(a) Who are the gainers from fashion trends?
(b) Who are the losers from fashion trends and why?
(c) Why are people so concerned about what they wear?

After about ten minutes ask the teams to report back.

Going further

What does the Bible have to say about what we wear? In groups, have the young people examine the Bible passages on the cards below. Then hold a discussion on how we should decide what to wear.

Card 1: Timothy 2:9–11
Card 2: Matthew 6:28–33
Card 3: Genesis 3:6–11
Card 4: Genesis 37:1–4

Firm foundations

Aim

To look at the basis of our decision making.

Equipment

True or False Sheets and Bible Cards (see below). One set of children's wooden bricks per team. An OHP or flipchart for sharing answers to the True or False Sheet.

Warm-up

Divide the group into teams of between four and seven members, and give each team a bucket of bricks. Tell them that they have five minutes to build the highest self-standing tower. After five minutes announce a winning team.

Main session

1. Give out a True or False Sheet to each person. They must each complete it by themselves. Exam conditions: no conferring, copying etc.!

True or false?

Write "T" or "F" in the space provided.

1. Love is blind. ____
2. If everyone says it, it must be true. ____
3. The moon is made of green cheese. ____
4. If it feels good, do it. ____
5. You cannot get pregnant the first time you have sex. ____
6. Money cannot buy you love. ____
7. Miracles do not happen today. ____

8. If it is worth having, it is worth the wait. ____
9. Blondes have more fun. ____
10. A little bit of what you fancy does you good. ____

2. When everyone has finished filling in the sheet, ask them to get into pairs and to share their answers and the reasons behind them. When they have done this for all ten questions, gather the pairs together and put the chart below on the OHP/flipchart:

Question	True	False	Facts	Faith	Feelings
1					
2					
3					
4					
5					
6					
7					
8					
9					
10					

3. Taking one question at a time, ask each pair whether they answered "true" or "false" and also whether their answer was based on:

(a) *Facts:* things which they know to be true. They can learn facts either from other people or else through their own experience and investigation.
(b) *Faith:* things which they believe to be true. Beliefs are based on evidence or testimony of trustworthy people.
(c) *Feelings:* things which they feel are true and right. Sometimes we feel that something is right when we have no evidence that it is right, or even when the evidence says it is wrong.

4. When the chart is filled in, ask the young people if they have any comments or observations to make.

5. Divide the group into three teams. Give each of the teams one of the Bible Cards below, and allow them about ten minutes to answer the questions.

Bible Card 1: Luke 7:46–49

* What is the foundation that we are to build on?
* Why do you think the foolish man built his house upon the sand?
* What is the equivalent today of building a house on sand?

Bible Card 2: Luke 14:28–30

* What is the foundation that we are to build on?
* Is there a cost involved when we build on this foundation?
* If so, what is it?

Bible Card 3: Luke 14:31–33

* Would the King be right to consider the cost of going to war?
* What is the cost of being a disciple for us today?

---

6. When the ten minutes are up call the group back together again and ask the teams to share their answers.

7. Give a simple talk along these lines: "We need to have a firm foundation to our Christian faith. We need a solid basis from which to make decisions about what is true and what is false. Here are some helpful guidelines for when you need to make decisions about things:

(a) Check out the facts. God has given you a brain and the ability to investigate things, so see if the facts add up.
(b) Check out the Scriptures. God's Word is trustworthy and reliable, so use it as a guide when making decisions.
(c) Check it out with an older Christian and listen to their advice. They may well be able to help with (a) and (b) above.
(d) Check it out with God. In your prayers ask Him to guide and advise you.

8. Close in prayer.

The gift auction

Aim

To look at how the young people value and prioritize talents and abilities, and to challenge the worldly attitude which says, "We are what we can do."

Preparation

Copy or adapt the gift catalogue below and make some home-made money.

Gift auction catalogue

Lot 1.	Good looks	Lot 16.	Strong voice
Lot 2.	Sense of humour	Lot 17.	Kindness
Lot 3.	Strength	Lot 18.	Strong will
Lot 4.	Good at languages	Lot 19.	Self-control
Lot 5.	Compassion	Lot 20.	Good eyesight

Lot 6. Athletic	Lot 21. Thin
Lot 7. Beauty	Lot 22. Self-confidence
Lot 8. Good figure	Lot 23. Gentleness
Lot 9. Musical gift	Lot 24. Outgoing
Lot 10. Intelligent	Lot 25. Creative
Lot 11. Artistic	Lot 26. Loving
Lot 12. Acting skill	Lot 27. Mechanical skill
Lot 13. Quick thinker	Lot 28. Faithfulness
Lot 14. Courageous	Lot 29. Wisdom
Lot 15. Charisma	Lot 30. Sociable

Action

1. There are two possible ways of holding the auction:

(a) Everyone is given some money and a copy of the catalogue. Without conferring with anyone, the players allocate to each gift the amount they want to bid for it. All the catalogues are collected and the gifts are given to those who have bid the most for them. The winning bid for each of the gifts is written on a flipchart/OHP, so that everyone can see which gifts are the most valuable and which have not had any bids. If you do the auction this way, there will be some young people who do not receive a single gift.

(b) Everyone is allocated money (either the same or different amounts each), and you run down the catalogue taking bids for each lot, with the highest bidder winning. Those who are out-bid can still use their money to bid for other items on the list.

Whichever way you do it, the auction will produce a list of the values placed on each of the gifts by the young people. It will also make those young people who failed to obtain the gifts they wanted feel frustrated and disappointed.

2. If you are a large group break into smaller cells, each with a leader, to discuss the following:

(a) What happened? Who got which gifts? Who got no gifts? etc.

(b) How did you feel about what happened? Was it fair or unfair?

(c) Were you surprised by which items were most valuable and least valuable?

(d) Do you think the auction accurately represented the values which society places on certain gifts? Do you think those values are right?

(e) Which gifts from this list did Jesus look for when He was choosing the disciples?

(f) Where does our value in God's eyes come from?

3. Draw the groups back together and let them share some of their answers. Then draw the meeting to a close. If it is appropriate, read 1 Corinthians 1:26 and talk about how God uses people who, according to society's value system, do not have what it takes to do great things for Him.

24-hour dilemma

Aim

To look at how the young people would cope in certain situations.

Equipment

A Dilemma Board (see below), a set of Dilemma Cards (ditto), dice, counters etc. (If the group is large you may need two sets of equipment.)

11 12 1
10 2

24
HOUR
DILE●MMA

1. When you land on a square choose either the a.m. or the p.m. Question/Dilemma
2. If one dilemma card has already been answered you get the other one.
3. If both have been answered you can throw again if you wish.

9 3

8 4

7 6 5

Dilemma Cards

7 a.m.   While on your paper round you notice that you are being followed by an unknown man.

8 a.m.   In your reading this morning from the Old Testament, God slays Israel's enemies, and you can't understand why God would do something like that.

9 a.m.   You were out late the night before and you know that if you don't get up now you won't make it to church.

10 a.m.   At school someone in your class is being bullied. You don't particularly like them, but what should you do?

11 a.m.	While in town you find a wallet with over £50 in it. What should you do?
12 noon	While cooking lunch you burn your hand on the cooker. No one else is home.
1 p.m.	You want to start a lunchtime Christian meeting at school, but you haven't got a room to meet in.
2 p.m.	While out clothes shopping with a friend he/she wants to buy something outrageous/provocative/ expensive.
3 p.m.	Some of your friends are meeting down at the arcade for an afternoon of video games.
4 p.m.	A group of friends meet for a smoke after school and invite you along.
5 p.m.	You're in a burger bar and one of your friends won't eat or drink anything. You realize it's weeks since you have seen them eating.
6 p.m.	The youth group are holding a barbecue but you are meant to be having tea with your grand-parents.
7 p.m.	One of your acquaintances from school has asked you to take him/her to the youth group, but they are not part of the crowd.
8 p.m.	You have some homework that has to be in the next day, but you would rather be doing some-thing else.
9 p.m.	Your parents are out and you are making yourself a cup of tea, when you smell gas in the kitchen.
10 p.m.	Your friends are all staying late at a party but you promised you would be home at 10 p.m.
11 p.m.	A friend comes round really upset because his/her parents are arguing and fighting again.
Midnight	You are at a sleepover when your friends decide to watch a video meant for adults only.
1 a.m.	Mum and Dad went out for a quick drink down the pub and haven't got back yet.

2 a.m.   You hear your Mum in tears because it would
           have been your Dad's birthday, but he died last
           year.

3 a.m.   You wake up because little brother is being sick.
           Mum's on the night shift and you know Dad has to
           be up early for work.

4 a.m.   You wake up frightened by nightmares and can't
           get back to sleep.

5 a.m.   Your older sister/brother, with whom you share a
           room, has an asthma attack.

6 a.m.   You wake early and are watching the dawn when
           you see a man climbing out of a nearby house's
           window.

How to play

1. Each player needs a token. They can start from any time in
the day or night.

2. The object is to cope with any crisis that you encounter.

3. The player throws the dice and moves the number of hours
round the board indicated by the dice.

4. The player turns up and reads the appropriate card for the
hour.

5. The player has to say what he/she would do in that situation.

6. When the player has finished the other players can challenge what he/she has said in two ways:

(a) They can say that the action which he/she has taken is the
incorrect action for that situation.

(b) They can say that it is not the action which the individual
would take in the situation.

7. When the person has replied to the challenge, move on to
the next player.

8. The game ends when time runs out or when all the situations have been dealt with.

Projects

Building an Advent Wall
Parents' Evening 1
Parents' Evening 2
Producing a Play or a Musical
Community Projects
Designing a Game
Strawberry Tea
Cake Auction
Disability Awareness

PROJECTS

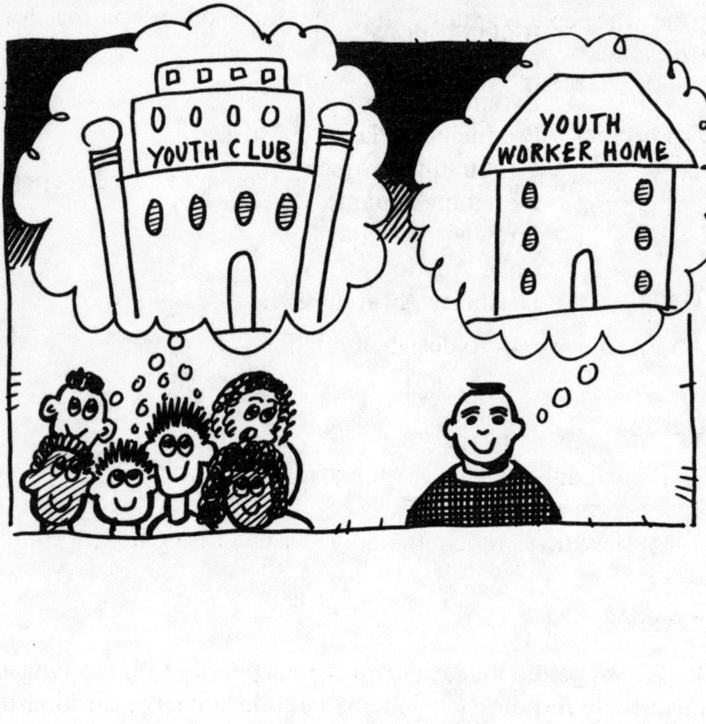

Building an Advent Wall

Aim

To provide an opportunity for young people to meet adults from the congregation, and to teach on preparing for Christmas.

Equipment

30 cardboard boxes, paint, masking tape, gaffa tape, paper, pencils etc.

Time

About four weeks to design and build.

Outline

1. Design and build an Advent Wall.
2. Position it in church.
3. Systematically open one door per day through Advent.

Action

1. We suggested the idea to our young people and, receivng a favourable response from them, we collected large cardboard boxes from local shops.
2. Each young person had to design an Advent scene to fit in the box. They also had to decide what shape and size the door in their box should be.

3. When the designs had been approved, the young people then started work on their boxes. Some of the designs were three-dimensional, others were two-dimensional.

4. In addition to the 24 Advent designs, a crib scene was put into another box.

5. The 25 boxes were painted with white emulsion on the outside and were then arranged as a wall, tapering towards the top. All the doors were shut, and then a huge Christmas tree with presents hanging on it was painted on the wall. When the painting was finished each of the doors was marked with the date on which it was to be opened.

6. We did not stick the boxes together at this stage, because we wanted the young people to bring them into church during a Sunday morning service and to assemble the wall there.

7. When the time comes to assemble the wall, it's a good idea to use double-sided tape to hold the boxes together. You can also get a very nice effect by inserting a string of Christmas tree lights through small holes made in the boxes.

8. With the wall finally assembled in church, the doors can now be opened. There are a number of ways of doing this:

(a) Open a week's worth on a Sunday morning.

(b) Find out what activities take place in the church during the week and arrange with the organizers of those activities to go along to their meetings and open the door for that particular day.

(c) Ask the church's key-holders if some of the young people can open a door in the wall after school each day.

9. The greater the link between the young people and the members of the congregation the better.

Hints

1. The project is easier if the boxes are all of a similar size.

2. Do use this activity as an opportunity to get the young people to read the Bible together, especially the accounts of Jesus' birth in Matthew's and Luke's Gospels. Talk about

what Jesus' arrival meant, what people's expectations were. Perhaps even dig into the prophets. Opportunities may well spontaneously arise to talk about the meaning of Advent, and it's good to be ready to use them.

Parents' evening 1

Aim

To introduce the parents to the style and methods of your youth group and to create opportunities for parent/young person interaction.

Preparation

Send the parents written invitations well in advance of the event. The young people will need to be well briefed.

Equipment

The equipment you normally use at your youth group meetings.

Warm-up

Use some ice-breakers to get everyone (both young people and parents) moving and mixing: e.g. Crazy Chase, Spaghetti Numbers and Human Dominoes from Chapter 7. Also see *Big Ideas for Small Youth Groups* and *Youthbuilders* for further ideas.

Main session

1. Ask everyone to form pairs – ideally, one young person with one parent.
2. Give a short introduction to the activity: "We are going to

do an exercise in listening. One of the hardest things in the Christian life is listening to God, so we are going to find out how good we are at listening to each other. One of you is 'A' and the other is 'B'. A is going to talk to B for two minutes about what they did on Thursday. B is to listen without interruption."

3. After two minutes ask them to swap over: B now tells A what he/she did last Thursday.

4. After another two minutes B has one minute to say what A did last Thursday. Then A has to say what B did. How much have they remembered? Were they really listening?

5. Ask the people to talk about which they found easiest – listening or talking. Make sure that neither adults nor young people dominate the discussion.

6. Pair each couple with another to form groups of four, and give each group one of the Bible Question Cards below:

Bible Question Cards

Card 1: Read 1 Kings 19:1–18
(a) In how many different ways did God speak to Elijah? What were those ways?
(b) God did not speak through the fire or the earthquake. Why do you think this was?
(c) What advice does the passage give us concerning listening to God today?

Card 2: Read John 1:35–38
(a) What did Jesus do in order to spend time with His Father?
(b) The disciples were not with Him. Why do you think this was?
(c) What can we learn from the passage about our own need for a time with God each day and how to achieve it?

Card 3: Read Psalm 17:1–9
(a) What are the characteristics of God that David mentions in his prayer?

(b) How has David prepared himself to come into God's presence?

(c) What can we learn from this to apply to our own times of prayer and waiting on God?

Let the groups have about 15 minutes to do the Bible investigation and then have a time of reporting back. Try to give all the groups an opportunity to say something. Then make some concluding comments and move into the next stage.

7. Divide the parents from the young people and put the two age groups into separate rooms to talk about their experiences. Have a member of the youth leadership with each group. Ask everyone to ensure that whatever is said remains confidential to the group.

Questions to talk about

(a) How did we feel about working together with the young people/adults?

(b) Were we surprised by what they said or did?

(c) What were the best things you discovered in working with the young people/adults?

(d) Is there one thing you would like to say to the young people/adults to encourage them in their Christian faith?

8. After they have had enough time to discuss these questions, draw the two groups back together. The two youth leaders now (sensitively) share what the groups said about each other.

9. End with hot drinks and biscuits or chips and cola etc.

Parents' evening 2

Aim

To meet with parents to explain to them the aims and objectives of the youth group. To develop relationships with them and to enable them to develop relationships with each other (without the young people being present).

Equipment

This depends on the style of the evening. You could offer the parents wine and cheese, or coffee and cakes, or beer and pork pies! Be culturally relevant to the parents being invited.

Preparation

Send out invitations well in advance so that people book the event in their diaries.

Action

1. Arrange the room according to the style of the event. It can be a good idea to get the youth group to make displays of the things they have been involved in, with photos or write-ups, or to show any things they have made etc. This gives the parents something to talk about while they mix.

2. When the parents arrive greet them. Arrange for other members of the youth team to serve food and drinks.

3. After about 20 minutes give a presentation about the youth group. Include the following points:

(a) What you do.
(b) Why you do it.
(c) Where your funds come from.
(d) When the residential weeks/weekends in the coming year will be.
(e) Why the residentials are helpful and important to the young people.
(f) What you will or will not inform parents of (e.g. would you or wouldn't you tell parents if you found their youngster smoking outside a youth group meeting?). It's important that this area is made clear.

4. Allow the parents to ask questions, but if they want to talk in more detail about individual young people, talk to them privately after the presentation.

5. Use the time after the presentation to talk to as many parents as possible. Try not to tell *them* all about *their* young people, but try instead to develop a relationship with them.
6. At the end of the evening get together with the other leaders to talk about any weaknesses that you need to work on or any strengths that were a source of encouragement.

Hints

Developing good relationships with non-church parents can have real advantages. Once we were desperate to borrow a car for a houseparty. No church parents would lend us one, but a non-church parent lent us a brand-new, expensive vehicle with the comment, "It's only a box on wheels." We find that whenever we spend time as a leadership getting to know a parent it works to everyone's advantage.

Producing a play or a musical

There are a variety of plays, musicals and dance dramas that are ideal for this age range and which could be put on with the resources of a youth group. For more details on how to produce a play or a musical read John Reaney's chapter in *Creative Ideas for Youth Evangelism* (HarperCollins).

Community projects

These are fun for the young people and enable them to help others. They are also one of the best ways of raising the profile of your youth group and building up a team spirit. Here are some of the ways in which young people can make their presence felt in the community:

Clearing gardens

In most congregations there are those who find that they can no longer manage their gardens. A team from your youth group could go round and cut the grass, weed the borders etc. If you want to operate outside the congregation, contact your local CAB or Help the Aged.

Litter picking

This is not the most pleasant of tasks! But Jesus said we are to be servants, and litter picking or tidying up an area of wasteland is a valuable service to the community. Check with the local council about who owns the land and make sure you have permission. Let parents know about it, and tell the local papers what you are doing.

Cleaning the church

Volunteer the youth group to spend a Saturday cleaning the church. Ask those who are responsible for the building to come and supervise. Provide the young people with a list of the materials and equipment they will need. Arrange a time, then get stuck into the grime! It's really important that the young people develop a servant heart; they need to see that the Christian faith is not all about "What I want".

Servant Squad

Hold a Servant Squad Day, when members of the congregation can ask the youth group to do any task, e.g. cleaning out the garage, washing the car, digging the veggie patch etc. They could do this for free, or they could ask for donations to youth group funds.

Sponsoring a child

This is one way of demonstrating our concern for our brothers and sisters in Christ in the Two Thirds World. However, child sponsorship has disadvantages as well as advantages. Speak to Tearfund to find out what is involved and what the pros and cons are.

Carol singing

A good way to raise a little cash. Many people are delighted to be visited by a group of real carol singers. You could give out information about Christmas services etc. A nice way to spread the good cheer is to sing some carols at an old people's home. They will enjoy the presence of the young people and the carols as well.

Design a game

Aim

For the youth group to design a game which will continue for several weeks and which will be an open challenge to the rest of the church.

Equipment

All the games equipment you have: balls, bats, stumps, hoops, skittles, chalk, string, nets etc. Large sheets of mounting card, coloured card, rulers, felt-tipped pens, pencils, stencils etc.

Warm-up

Divide the group into teams of between four and six and give each team a selection of items from the games equipment.

Their task is to design a new game to be played by two, three or four teams at a time. The teams have 20 minutes to design and practise their games. Then the whole group plays the games one at a time. After this ask the young people which game they have enjoyed the most. Make a note of this and play it at regular intervals through the term.

Main session

1. Form pairs or small groups and ask them to design a board game. They may need some help, but we have found that young people can be highly imaginative, and some of the games they create are quite complex.

2. Steps for the pairs/small groups to follow:

(a) Think of all the board games you like. Why do you like them? How do they work? Do they use dice, cards, money etc.? What is the board like?

(b) Think of some fun ideas to base games on.

(c) Sort through the ideas and choose one that will work well.

(d) Draw the board for your game on paper and play it with your small group to see if it works. Make any necessary changes and then play it again.

(e) When you are happy with your game, explain it to the leaders and tell them what equipment you will need to make it.

(f) Manufacture the board, pieces, cards, equipment etc. to the best of your ability.

3. When all the groups have made their games, spend an evening playing them all, seeing which ones prove popular.

4. Invite all the members of the congregation to come and play the young people's games. It will be a fun evening and a good opportunity for people to get to know each other. End the evening with light refreshments.

Strawberry tea

Aim

To integrate the young people with the adults in the congregation. This activity is also a good way of raising money for youth group funds.

Equipment

Tables, table-cloths, table decorations, chairs, crockery, cutlery, invitations and tickets.

Preparation

Advertise the event, making sure that it doesn't clash with other church events. Book the hall as a wet-weather option. The young people will need to know what to do and how to do it, e.g. which tables they are responsible for serving, what is being served, what to wear etc. Those involved in the entertainment will need to practise. Menus will have to be drawn up and copied off. It is best to sell tickets in advance and to have a flat-rate charge for the event. This helps by giving you an idea of how many people will come and by providing you with some cash for the purchase of strawberries, cream, milk etc.

Action

1. Select a day for the event in the strawberry season. A Sunday afternoon is probably best, but a Saturday could work just as well.
2. Arrange for the youth group to make sandwiches and cakes to bring along. Alternatively they could bring the ingredients and make up the sarnies at the hall.
3. Some of the young people will need to go to a local pick-your-own farm to pick the strawberries.
4. Some of your group members should be given the job of

setting up the tables on the church lawn where the tea party is to be held. They could also put up some bunting. You will need some willing workers to do the washing up! (It can be a good idea to work on a rota system, to make sure everyone has a go at everything.)

5. At the end of the day thank all the young people for their efforts. Work out how much money the event has raised and announce the final figure.

Cake auction

Aim

This is both a fund-raiser and an opportunity for the young people to be integrated with the adult church members and the wider community.

Equipment

Entry forms.

Preparation

1. Book the event in the church calendar.
2. Publicize the event in the church magazine or the local press.
3. Ask a local celebrity or a professional chef to judge the cakes, and also ask someone with the gift of the gab to be the auctioneer!

Action

1. The youth group challenges people to enter a grand cake-making competition. There can be a number of categories.

E.g.:
(a) Children Under Ten
(b) Superior Sponge
(c) Men Only
(d) Youth Group Challenge
(e) Icing Extravaganza
Design the categories to fit your situation.

2. To enter a person has to pick up an entry form from the youth group. There is a nominal fee of 10p per entry. All cakes entered are the property of the youth group.

3. It's best to hold the event in your church hall after a Sunday morning service. Cakes need to be delivered to the church hall either on the Saturday night or on the Sunday morning before the service. Make sure that an entry form bearing the competitor's details is with each cake.

4. Your chef/celebrity judges the entries and awards first, second and third prizes in each category. Then he/she should announce as the overall winner the competitor who has entered the best cake out of all the categories. If you're planning to hold a cake auction annually, have a cup made for the overall winner.

5. Finally auction off all the cakes to raise some money for your youth group funds.

Disability awareness

Aim

To raise the group's awareness of disabled people and to develop links with them.

Preparation

You will need to book activities and make arrangements well in advance.

Action

Many different activities are possible, depending on what facilities are available in your area. Here are some ideas:

1. *Wheelchair basketball*. There are a number of organizations serving the disabled which will cooperate with your group in this activity. Arrange for the use of a local sports hall, where the young people can play wheelchair basketball with the disabled people. This will give the group a good opportunity to mix with them, ask questions and get to know them.

2. *Shopping centre visit*. Arrange a visit to your local shopping centre, but with a difference. Have some of the young people in wheelchairs, others blindfolded, others using walking frames etc. Divide them into small groups and give them a variety of tasks to undertake, e.g. visit a bank, buy a shirt, have a burger, find out what's on at the cinema, post a letter etc.

When the group have returned to base get them to talk about what they did. How did people respond to them? How did they feel at different stages of the exercise? How do they feel now? What have they learned? etc.

3. *Group visit*. Arrange to visit a group or centre for the mentally handicapped. Depending on the leaders, it may be possible for you to sing songs, do drama and play a few games as well as chat with and get to know the group/centre members. They might want to return the visit. Our local Gateway Club used to send a group along to our evening youth service. They really enjoyed it, and we enjoyed having them as well. The free and uninhibited way in which they worshipped was an inspiration to us.

4. *Day out*. Contact the local organizations serving the disabled and discuss with them the idea of organizing a joint day out for your group and some disabled people. Even better, get some young people from both groups to talk through the options and possibilities. The process of learning and developing relationships through action is the key.

4

Social Events

Introduction

Food ideas
Disguised Dinner
Banana Binge
Spaghetti Spectacular
Progressive Meals
Marshmallow Mania

Theme events

Now the Good News
Non-Halloween Party
Firework Party
Balloon Bonanza

Shoot-Out Spectacular
Those Were the Years
Incredible Sleepover
Green Party

Out and about socials
Crazy Car Rally
Swim Barbecue
Sport for All
Go-Karting
Dragon Boat Racing
Boat Trip

Golden oldie socials

SOCIAL EVENTS

Holy Trinity youth gave thanks for the conversion of a local chef.

INTRODUCTION

Social events serve a variety of useful purposes within the youth group. Therefore a regular and varied social programme is often a very helpful addition to the discipleship programme.

Social events give the leaders the opportunity to talk to the young people in an informal setting where the young people feel more comfortable and where the leaders have more time to chat.

The young people can invite their non-Christian friends along to a social event. This will show the friends that many of their ideas about Christian groups are ill-founded. (Of course, we are assuming here that the group members have non-Christian friends to invite along. However, many Christian young people do not have any non-Christian friends. We need to be aware of this when planning events.)

Social events are fun! It is important that young people have the opportunity to talk and chat, enjoy themselves and learn inter-personal skills in a friendly environment. They need to see that this is an integral part of Christianity: that fun and God are not incompatible!

Social events can assist the development of group identity by giving the members shared common experiences. This can give the young people a sense of belonging. As a result new members will be drawn into the group, because they want that same sense of belonging. (We need, however, to be aware of the danger of the group becoming a clique, with too many shared experiences and not enough openness to outsiders.)

The ideas below are not a definitive list of suggestions – they are merely some fun ideas which I have collected over the years. Some of them involve food and can therefore be quite expensive. To avoid over-burdening the youth group budget (if you have one!), and also to prevent the group from developing a non-Christian view of food, it is best not to do too many food-centred events.

FOOD IDEAS

Disguised dinner

Aim

To have a fun social event which the young people can invite their friends to and which provides an opportunity for intimacy and the development of adult roles. It is also an opportunity for the leaders to develop their cooking skills(!) and to actively serve the young people.

Form

A meal cooked and served by the leaders, with printed menus. Arrange the room as a formal restaurant, and dress accordingly. The catch is that the menus are written in code: the items are not easily identifiable!

Equipment

Plates, bowls, side-plates, cutlery etc. Tables, table-cloths, candles, napkins, flowers – in fact anything which helps to create a sophisticated atmosphere. Menu cards and order forms. And, of course, the food!

Preparation

1. Produce some invitation cards and give them to the youth group members several weeks in advance. Ask them to bring along someone of the opposite sex.
2. Design the menu and produce some menu cards and order forms (see below).
3. Buy the food.
4. Iron your best black trousers or skirt and blow the dust off your bow-tie. Result: one smart youth leader!

Action

1. On the night, lay out the room to resemble a high-class restaurant, with a classical string quartet playing over the ghetto-blaster!
2. Try to get some extra helpers – perhaps parents or older young people – as the dishing up of the food in the right combinations is harder than it looks.
3. Cook the food so that it can all be kept warm or cold until it is time to serve it. Ensure that the young people do not see the choice of food that is available, or the mystery element of the event will be ruined.
4. Give each person a menu card and an order form:

DISGUISED DINNER MENU CARD

Tea Ship	Rather Smooth
Soft Scoop	Completely Mad
Yule Yell	Neptune's Kit
Hard Stuff	Wrecked Car
Thin & Flat	Tongue Teaser
Montecarlos	Sweet and Sticky
Junction Place	Thin Supporter
Sweet Canadian	Cat's Eye

Each item on the menu is either a food or an eating utensil.

ORDER FORM

Please state in the spaces below which items off the menu you
would like served for each course:

Starter	*Main course*
(a)	(a) ....
(b)	(b) ....
(c)	(c) ....
(d)	(d) ....

Dessert	*Afters*
(a)	(a) ....
(b)	(b) ....
(c)	(c) ....
(d)	(d) ....

5. Here is a decoded version of the menu:

Tea Ship = cutter = knife
Soft Scoop = butter
Yule Yell = I'll scream
   = ice cream
Hard Stuff = cheese
Thin & Flat = knife
Montecarlos = chips
Junction Place = fork
Sweet Canadian = maple
   syrup

Rather Smooth = spoon
Completely Mad = crackers
Neptune's Kit = fork
Wrecked Car = banger
   = sausage
Tongue Teaser = spoon
Sweet & Sticky = cherry
Thin Supporter = fan wafer
Cat's Eye = melon slice

You might like to think of other items and coded names to
include. This is an activity that can easily be reworked to fit
your own situation.
6. Well, as with every meal, afterwards it's washing up time!

Banana binge

All sorts of games can be played with bananas! Why not have a whole evening of banana activities? Send out banana-shaped party invitations, and tell everyone that they have to come in yellow clothes!

Banana Bobbing

Fill a baby bath or paddling pool with water. Throw in one banana for each person present. Divide the group into two teams. One at a time, the team members run up and remove a banana from the pool using their teeth only. The winning team is the first one whose members all have bananas.

Banana Volleyball

Use normal volleyball rules, except that the "ball" is a large inflated banana-shaped balloon. These are about a metre long and are available at many shops. Trying to hit the banana in a straight line will drive the players nuts!

Banana Darts

You will need an old dart-board and some thin masonry nails. Carefully hammer the nails through the dart-board from the back, so that the tips protrude at the front. Then hang the board up and play darts as normal, including the throwing action. No sideways lobbing of bananas is allowed!

Banana Stuff

Some volunteers sit at the front. They have to put peeled bananas in to their mouths without chewing or swallowing them. After inserting each banana they have to say, "I'm bananas about bananas!" The person who gets the most in and is still able to say the phrase wins.

Banana Fizz

Some volunteers go to the front to drink a can of Coke/Pepsi/7
Up and eat a banana. The first one to finish both is the winner.

Drawing the Short Banana

Make up a large bowl of banana whip. Put in several bananas
so that their ends are sticking out. Some of the bananas need
to be whole, others should be cut in half. The players in turn
come up and draw out a banana with their teeth. If they get a
whole one they must eat it; if they get a half they must do a
banana forfeit. You'll need to think up some forfeits appropriate to your group.

Banana Strings

You've probably played the spoon game where you tie a
spoon to the end of a long piece of string and pass it through
the inside of everyone's clothes. Instead of the spoon use a
banana, and also tie on some other bananas at regular intervals along the string.

Banana Quick Draw

Two contestants face each other with a banana tucked into
their belt or pocket. On the command "Go!" they have to
draw, peel and eat the banana, using only one hand. The first
to do so is the winner.

As you can see, almost every game can be adapted to include
bananas! If the Banana Binge becomes an annual event you'll
soon develop loads of fun activities and traditions. Finish off
the evening with banana splits and banana milkshakes.

Spaghetti spectacular

Spaghetti is great fun for youth group social events. Organize an evening of spaghetti activities. Encourage everyone to come dressed in Italian-type clothes. Send out invitations written on lasagne . . . the possibilities are endless!

Spaghetti Towers

Divide the group into teams of four. Give each team some spaghetti and some bubble gum. The task is to build the highest tower in 15 minutes, using only the materials given. Hint: the more the gum is chewed, the harder it sets.

Spaghetti Names

Using "Alphabetti Spaghetti" everyone has to write their name and address on a large sheet of paper.

Spaghetti Polo Pass

Divide the group into teams of equal size. Each player has a short length of dry spaghetti which is held in the mouth. Each team stands in a line. The object is to pass a Polo from one player to another on the spaghetti. The last player in each team places the Polo in a cup. Then he/she goes to the front of the line and passes it on again, until the new last player gets it. He/she then goes to the front of the line . . . and so on. The first team to rotate through all its players is the winner. No hands allowed!

Spaghetti Jackstraws

As normal Jackstraws, but use spaghetti.

Spaghetti Hair-do

Divide the group into boy/girl couples. Using cooked spaghetti, the girls redesign the lads' hair. The best (or worst?) new style wins!

Spaghetti Rope

The object is to make a self-supporting rope out of spaghetti. Hold both ends off the ground to check that it is self-supporting before announcing a winner.

Spaghetti Chew

Couples start eating on either end of a piece of cooked spaghetti. The first couple to finish wins.

Adapt other games for spaghetti, or see if the young people have any ideas. At the end of the evening finish with anything, but not spaghetti!

Progressive meals

These are known under a variety of different names, such as tramps' suppers. The central idea is that different parts of a meal are served at different locations, and everyone walks/drives/roller-skates between venues. Try a few variations:

Progressive Sandwich Construction

The bread at the first venue, the marge at the second and fillings at subsequent venues, so that at the end you have a very sweaty chewed sarnie. Great fun!

Progressive Slaves' Supper

The youth group all do chores at each of the venues and are then served bread and water at the finish. They'll love that one!

Progressive Pancake Munch

A frying pan, fat and eggs are collected at the first venue, milk and flour at the second and fillings at the third. Dash to the final venue to make and eat the pancakes. As a variation, this can be done in teams at different venues. The first team to cook and eat their pancakes and do their washing up are the winners!

Progressive Shared Supper

The youth group arrange to meet in the homes of several church families. At each house they cook a course of the meal and share it with the family concerned, and then move on to the next house. The families get a meal cooked for them, but they have to share it with hordes of youths!

Progressive Pizza Build

Start with the base and add a topping to it at each venue.

Marshmallow mania

A wonderful opportunity to play all those disgusting food games you never get the chance to play normally, e.g. drinking Coke through a sock, sucking liquorice boot-laces out of instant whip, licking cream off balloons suspended on elastic . . . you name it, you can do it! Pick the wildest, wackiest events you can think of. Use volunteers only for the up-front games. Play plenty of team food games as well, so everyone can join in.

For instance, marshmallows are really not the sort of things that diet-conscious adults eat, but for some reason young people love them. So, for an evening of mania decorate the room with anything pink or white and play all the usual marshmallow games, such as:

Crazy Mallow Golf

Use buckets, dustpans, boxes etc. to create a series of crazy golf holes. The marshmallows are the golf balls, and use hockey sticks as the clubs. It's best to play this game outside.

Mallow Dragsters

Each team has to build the ultimate dragster, using marshmallows, cocktail sticks, cotton and cardboard wheels. After they are all constructed have a contest in which the winner is the one which travels furthest. Use a plank leaning against a chair as a launch ramp.

Spiny Mallow

The group is divided into two teams and each person is given a cocktail stick. With the sticks placed in their mouths and without using their hands, each team has to pass a mallow from person to person, each one leaving his/her stick stuck in. As each stick is added, it gets harder to add another. The first team to pass the mallow right down the line is the winner.

Chubby Bunnies

An old favourite. Contestants have to stuff marshmallows into their mouths and say "Chubby bunnies!" after inserting each one. The contestant with the most in his/her mouth is the winner. (Have a bucket handy!)

Finish the evening either with hot chocolate with mallows in it or with ice cream and melted mallows.

THEME EVENTS

Now the Good News

Newspaper games are great fun and don't put a strain on the youth group budget. A Newspaper Evening could include Newspaper Fashion Design, Newspaper Couples (see *Youthbuilders*, p. 40) and Beat the Stick (see *Youthbuilders*, p. 44). Here are some more ideas:

Deadly Newsprint

Place a large sheet of open newspaper on the floor. Everyone holds hands in a circle round it. Anyone treading on the newspaper is out, and if two players break hands they are both out. The objective is to be the last player still in.

Blind Strip

An up-front game. Blindfold three contestants and give them each a sheet of newspaper. They have one minute to produce the longest continuous strip of paper. (It isn't easy to do when you're blindfolded!)

What's in the News

Each person is given a couple of pages from various newspapers. Two notice boards are put up at opposite ends of the room. One is for the "Good News" and the other for the "Bad News". Everyone has to rip up their newspaper pages and stick each piece to the appropriate board. Divide the group into pairs: everyone has three minutes to decide why the media concentrate on the bad news rather than the good, and then to think of one piece of good news from the last few days to stick on the "Good News" board. Talk about the good news that Jesus offers.

Non-Hallowe'en party

Unfortunately there is today a renewed interest in the occult, and it is therefore important that we provide positive, enjoyable Christian alternatives to the celebration of evil. It is not enough nowadays just to ignore Hallowe'en: it is far better to face up to it and defeat it. We need to counteract the destructive nature of Hallowe'en by emphasizing light, life, creativity and the love and goodness of God.

Activities

1. *Praise and worship*. A mixture of popular praise that this age will enjoy can be a good component of the evening, with everyone dancing and clapping.
2. *Games*. Organize some team games, co-operative games with prizes and an element of risk, excitement, hilarity and fun.
3. *Fireworks*. As Hallowe'en is near to Firework Night, you might like to finish the evening with a display.
4. *Input*. Use the games, the gaps between the songs etc., to put forward not only the facts about Christianity but also a positive attitude towards fun. It is important, however, to keep the spiritual input light – Hallowe'en is not the best night for a biblical exposition on the nature of demons!

Firework party

One of the first ever Christian events that I got invited to, as a heathen, was my sister's Pathfinder Firework Party. Why not hold an annual church firework event? The youth group can prepare the food, make the bonfire, plan the entertainment etc. while the rest of the congregation come along for a good time. A couple of responsible adults are needed to sort out the fireworks.

Some good games and activities are: bonfire toffee, soup, toffee apples, bobbing for apples, the chocolate game, the spoon on the string game (see Banana Binge in this chapter), jacket potatoes, hot punch . . . All of this mixes together the old and the young, church and non-church people etc. Great fun!

Balloon bonanza

Balloons are a standard part of any youth leader's survival kit. An evening of balloon-based activities is a must. Balloons provide opportunities for uninhibited and unthreatening interaction.

As the young people arrive give them a balloon which has their name written on it and a piece of paper inside. On the paper is written the name of an animal, e.g. lion, elephant, rhino etc. Each piece of paper has a twin with the same animal name on it. When everyone has arrived they have to burst their balloons without using their hands or any sharp objects. Without showing anyone their piece of paper or making any noise, the players have to find the other person in the group with the same animal name.

Here are some more ideas for balloon games:

Balloon Water Toss

Each pair of young people has one water-filled balloon. They stand nose to nose outside. The first person in each pair takes a step back and gently throws the balloon to his/her partner. On catching the balloon, that player also takes a step back and throws the balloon back to the first player – and so on . . . The object of the game is to be the pair who throw the balloon the longest distance without it bursting.

Armpit Balloon Wrestle

Two champions are selected for an up-front game. Place a water-filled long balloon under each of the contestants' armpits. The contestants link fingers and try to burst their opponent's balloons without having their own burst.

Balloon Hugging

An old favourite and a game that everyone can play. Divide the group into pairs and give each pair a balloon. The balloon is placed between the couple, who stand face to face, and the object is simply to hug each other until the balloon bursts.

Balloon Headbangers

An up-front game for three volunteers. Each wears a baseball hat with a mapping pin, point upwards, taped to the middle of the hat. Blindfold the volunteers and hang three water-filled balloons six inches above their heads. The object is for each volunteer to burst his/her balloon. The audience yell instructions to guide the volunteers to their targets and encourage them in their jumping.

Finish off the evening with cold refreshments.

Shoot-out spectacular

Young people love water-fights. Any excuse for one, and they will be soaking each other happily. Invite everyone along and tell them to bring their own water-pistols. Have a deputy on the door to collect all the pistols as the people arrive. Play some shoot-out games:

Squirt Hunt

A loaded water-pistol is placed between two blindfolded players. They have to try to find it and squirt the other player first.

Candle Shoot-Out

A row of lighted candles are placed on a table. From behind a line drawn an appropriate distance away, players in turn have to see how many candles they can extinguish with one gunful of water.

Quick-draw

Two contestants each have a water-pistol and a lighted candle which is a set distance away. The first one to shoot out his/her candle is the winner. Have several rounds to find a champion.

Fill the Cup

Divide the group into two teams of no more than eight. Each team selects a volunteer, who has a paper cup placed on the top of his/her head, suitably secured with elastic. Each team then stands in a circle around their paper cup. Both teams are given a bucket of water from which they may fill their water-pistols when they are empty. On the command "Go!" the teams have to squirt as much water as they can into the paper cup on their volunteer's head. After a few minutes measure the water, and the team with the most wins.

End the evening with plenty of time to spare. Give each person back their own water-pistol and encourage them to have a water-fight outside – not that they'll need much encouraging!

Those were the years

The music industry is constantly re-running the music of the 80s, 70s, 60s and even 50s, thus providing a plethora of opportunities for youth group theme evenings. Young people come dressed in the appropriate clothes, listen to the appropriate music and eat the appropriate food, and the hall has been decorated in the appropriate way (usually because it hasn't been decorated since then anyway!). These events are informal, good to invite people to and loads of fun.

The incredible sleepover adventure

The "sleepover" is one of the most incorrectly named events in the youth group dictionary, because when you get a group of young people trying to sleep in the same place at the same time sleep comes a long way down the priority list!

The ingredients for a good sleepover are some exciting activities to start the evening, followed by an excellent choice of games and/or videos. Also have ready a number of possible conversation starters for later in the evening, when the chat turns from its usual topics to more serious subjects.

It is important to have adult male and female leaders at this event. Provide separate-sex rooms for those who want or need their sleep. Encourage everyone to get at least a little sleep!

Green Party

With the environment rarely out of the news these days, why not have a Green Party? Send out invitations on recycled paper or on the reverse side of junk mail. Deliver these either on foot or by bike. Everyone has to wear as much green as possible. Here are some green games to play at the party:

Signature Bingo Link Up

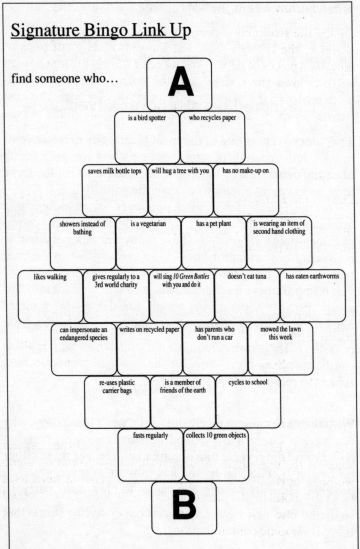

find someone who…

A

is a bird spotter	who recycles paper

saves milk bottle tops — will hug a tree with you — has no make-up on

showers instead of bathing — is a vegetarian — has a pet plant — is wearing an item of second hand clothing

likes walking — gives regularly to a 3rd world charity — will sing *10 Green Bottles* with you and do it — doesn't eat tuna — has eaten earthworms

can impersonate an endangered species — writes on recycled paper — has parents who don't run a car — mowed the lawn this week

re-uses plastic carrier bags — is a member of friends of the earth — cycles to school

fasts regularly — collects 10 green objects

B

Rules
1. Try to link A to B by any route by finding people who meet the description and sign the square.
2. You can only use the same signature once.
3. All signatures must be legible.

Wheelbarrow Muesli Munch

Divide the group into teams. In each team one person is the wheeler, the rest are barrows. Lay out a series of piles of muesli on pieces of paper. The wheeler wheels the first human barrow down the course, and the barrow eats the museli. They return to the team, and then the wheeler takes the next barrow down the course. The first team to eat all the museli piles wins.

Energy-Saving Relay

Players have to have at least three of their hands and feet (if you see what I mean) in contact with the ground at any one time. The first player to carry a mug of water from one end of the room to the other without cheating is the winner.

Recycling Game

Give each team a rubbish bag full of bits and pieces (e.g. string, sellotape, pieces of wood, old nuts and bolts, yogurt pots etc.). Their task is to make a useful object with it all! It can be anything they like – let their imaginations run riot. After ten minutes judge the winners.

The Muesli Bar Game

Each player in turn throws a die, and if it is a six they can eat some of the muesli bar – but first they have to put on some wellingtons (i.e. the rising sea level) and a pair of sunglasses (i.e. the hole in the ozone layer), and they have to feed someone else first before they can have any, to check that there is no toxic contamination!

Un-nature Trail

Lay out a walk through a garden or a wild space and see how many things people can spot that should not be there. Position a few beforehand to ensure that there are a good number.

Finish off the evening with green food, green lemonade, green cakes etc. (add food colouring).

Out and about socials

Crazy Car Rally

Aim

A fun activity and integration event.

Equipment

Maps and a set of clues.

Preparation

Plan the car rally. Give the congregation notice in advance that the young people may ask them to drive for them.

Action

1. Ask all the young people to get into teams of three.
2. Announce that in two weeks we are having a car rally, the winner of which will win a mega prize!
3. As none of your group members will be old enough to drive they will have to find people willing to drive them around. Tell them that they cannot ask anyone from their own

family or from the families of their fellow team members. They can only ask church members, but they can't ask any of the youth leaders.

4. Find out who is driving whom. If some of the young people are having problems finding a driver, have a few willing drivers whom the young people can contact.

5. The young people have to perform a series of tasks at different locations or solve a series of clues. The drivers are to follow the young people's instructions and are not to take the lead.

6. The drivers are not allowed to break the speed limit!

7. The winning team is the first one back with all the answers correct or the one to have completed the most when time is up.

8. Finish off with shared eats and drinks and give the prize to the winning team.

Swim Barbecue

This social event combines two popular youth group activities. Hire the local outdoor swimming pool for a Saturday evening. Lay on a barbecue (charge a set price for the whole event). Add other attractions such as a velcro wall and sumo suits. The latter are inflatable suits that make total weeds look like they have the body of a sumo wrestler! The two players have to try to bounce each other out of a circle. This is a great opportunity for the young people to bring along friends. Arrange some water activities as well – e.g. inflatables, silly games etc. – and the evening will be a total success.

Sport for All

Gone are the days when local sports centres offered a choice of five-a-side football, basketball or badminton. They often offer a wide range of events and activities and will arrange a programme to suit your group for a very reasonable price. This can include activities like:

Roller Hockey

This mix of unihoc and roller skating is fast and bruising but great fun.

Aero Ball

The most popular game at the time of writing with our 11 to 14s. It is a mix of basketball and trampolining played on a circular trampoline with four players on at a time. Ten-minute stints is about right and keeps everyone moving. It's totally exhausting!

Archery

This will need proper supervision, but if you book well in advance centres will lay this on.

Climbing walls

These vary from the simple to the extremely advanced. It is best to have instructors with you, for safety and so that the most can be made of the facilities.

Volleyball

A good team game. It is useful as a warm-up and to use as a filler for other activities.

Short Tennis

Played indoors with a soft foam ball and plastic rackets. It's a fun, simple version of tennis that builds up young people's confidence, and it's also good for coordination. The game also evens up the young people's size and strength variations.

Trampolining

Another instructed activity. It's great fun for leaders as well as members. The instructors should involve everyone and develop the activity over the session.

Work-out programmes

A mix of physical activities designed to suit the group.

Pirates

The old school game where two pirates are "it" and they have to tag the rest of the players, but no one is allowed to touch the ground. Players use ropes, bars, benches, climbing frames etc.

Competitive team sports

Lads really enjoy them at this age, and so arranging games against other youth groups can be a good way of attracting and keeping members as well as building up group identity and teamwork. Although there is a case against too much competitive sport in clubs, providing that the balance is OK, it can be a net positive.

Go-karting

The number of venues that offer Go-Karting for young people is steadily increasing. The price, though fairly high, is coming down, and some centres offer special prices for youth groups to fill off-peak times. The best source of information will be your local youth office, but also try any large Christian residential centres nearby, because some have Go-Karts and may lay on activities for non-resident groups.

Dragon boat racing

This strange-sounding activity is available at our local Scout water-sport activity centre. So to find out if it is available in your area, and if it isn't, what strange things might be available instead, contact your local Scout Association.

Boat trip

Several options are possible here, from punting followed by a picnic to a day out on a narrow boat learning how to operate locks and taking in the sun. You could hire some rowing boats on the local river or lake. As with any activity where there is a risk, make sure that every precaution is taken: have fun but be careful.

GOLDEN OLDIE SOCIALS

Barn dance
Ten-pin bowling
Theatre
Ice-skating
Night hike
Traffic-light tea
Beach barbecue
Picnic (in a crazy place!)
Cinema
Leisure pool

All the above are tried and tested for social events. They range from those which need a little organizing to those which are as spontaneous as you would like them to be. Don't forget that the good old-fashioned cinema trip can still be great fun.

Art & Craft Activities

ART+CRAFT ACTIVITIES

A subject generally glossed over.

Introduction

Art and craft activities are often an integral part of work with 11 to 14s. They provide great opportunity for teaching as well as for the young people to develop skills in teamwork, preparation and planning, perspective and concentration.

Art and craft materials are never cheap, so here are some tips for making the most of a limited budget:

Economy art tips

1. Store materials carefully, ensuring that they are usable next time.
2. Buy materials through the county purchasing organization.
3. Ask congregation members for any unwanted materials that can be used for art and craft. Issue a list of the sort of things you need.
4. Visit recycling centres on a regular basis, building up your supplies.
5. Plan ahead so that you don't have to buy from expensive local art shops.
6. Ask local businesses to help: e.g. a pottery could supply clay far more cheaply than anyone else, and they would fire it for a nominal fee.

Modroc fun

Modroc is groovy stuff that no worker with 11 to 14s should be without. It is plaster bandage and can be used for a multitude of activities.

Modroc Masks

Built on to wire frames or balloons. They dry much more quickly than papier mache, so they can be made and painted in a single evening. Use this activity to teach on life masks: i.e. people pretend to be one thing, when they are really something different inside.

Modroc Arms

Each person covers one of his/her arms with Vaseline so that the Modroc doesn't stick permanently. Wrap Modroc bandages on the arm downwards. When they have hardened, gently ease the cast off so that it remains intact. Paint it as lifelike as possible. Using more Modroc, mount all the arms on a board so that they are holding a globe. Use this visual aid to teach on how God has made us stewards of His world, and that we are responsible for its care and upkeep.

Modroc Boulder

Make a Modroc boulder and use it to teach that God calls us to work as a team together. On our own we can never achieve a fraction of what is possible together.

Modroc Scavenger Hunt

Give the teams supplies of Modroc, Vaseline and water and a list of items that they have to make plaster casts of.

Tie dyeing

As this is being written tie-dyed items are coming back into fashion. So it may be a trendy thing to convert boring white T-shirts into purple and green psychedelic designs.

As well as buckets, dyes, string and stones, a supply of practice cloths is always helpful. Alternatively use elastic bands instead of string and freezer bags instead of buckets. You will need two teaspoons of dye, two teaspoons of salt and a pint of water per person if you are using bags, so that each packet of dye will colour six shirts.

Use an old sheet or a large piece of material to produce a group design. This could then be the background for a banner bearing either Scripture verses or the youth group name/logo.

Edible collages

Collages are great fun and young people love making them. But what do you do with them when the evening is over, especially if the young people don't want to take them home? After many years of storing them in the youth group cupboard and having an annual clear-out, we came up with the ultimate solution: let the young people eat them!

To prevent a drastic drop in numbers the following week, edible collages require slightly different ingredients than normal ones.

Two decisions to make: is your collage going to be sweet or savoury, and is it going to be two- or three-dimensional?

For a basic two-dimensional edible collage you will need: rice paper, sugar glue (dissolve as much sugar as you can in half a litre of water, heat it, then allow it to cool), coloured sherbet, food colouring, paint-brushes (clean and sterile), icing sugar and coloured sugars.

For a more three-dimensional collage add other ingredients – icing, sweets, cake decorations, marzipan etc. – but they will need to be displayed flat.

Ideas for collages:

1. Make a collage of your moods: your opinion of yourself, how others see you etc. Use this as an opportunity for sharing about oneself.
2. Collages of how God sees you.
3. Collages of how we see God – what His character is like etc.
4. Collages of a Bible scene or an incident in Jesus' life.

Rock painting

Gather a collection of good-sized rocks and spread them out on newspaper. Each member of the group chooses one that is like him/herself. Share round the group why each person has chosen the rock that they have. Ask the group to think about their character and moods, and to paint their rock with the moods they experience and how they see their character. A PVA paint mix helps the paint to stick better. When everyone has finished let them introduce their rock and answer questions about it.

You could go on to say that God creates us all differently, and that our feelings and characters are unique.

Glass engraving

There are now a number of glass-engraving craft kits on the market. Put this together with all the free tankards and glasses that the petrol stations are always offering and you have the ideal combination for a Father's Day present.

Acquire enough tankards or glasses for one each and to have a few spare in case of accidents. On paper, the young people need to work out the designs they would like to etch onto the glass. When the designs are ready, etch them onto the glass using the kit. The kits come in two sorts – chemical and mechanical. Use the one that is the most appropriate to your youth group.

Clay

Clay is great fun to play with, and young people enjoy its feel and texture as well as making things with it. The only problem with it is that it can be messy. Don't allow the young people to throw it at each other or at the ceiling etc. Try to keep it on the work-surfaces.

If you don't want a selection of "undesirable" objects made, it is good to give the young people direction. Some suggestions would be:

1. Biblical objects: pots, lamps (which you could test to see if they work), bowls etc. Get a few Bible encyclopedias with plenty of pictures in to give the young people some ideas.
2. A youth group shield or coat of arms that has on it designs that symbolize the different ingredients of the group.
3. The young people's own tomb-stone in miniature, with an epitaph.

Whatever you make, if the young people want to keep it, try to have it fired. If they don't want to keep it, put the clay back and seal the bag properly to use another day. All the above ideas could stimulate discussion.

Paint

Every youth group uses paint, but there are ways of being inventive even with something as commonplace as paint. Here are some ideas:

Murals

Think big! See if the youth group can paint a mural. You might be able to do this directly onto a wall. Alternatively, cover the whole of the wall with paper and paint the mural on the paper.

Roll-on painting

Use roll-on deodorant containers full of paint. It's like using giant felt-tipped pens. Use them to do graffiti art or posters, or have a cartoon drawing competition with them.

Splatter painting

This is great fun in the summer months, when it can be done outside and there is no danger of walls and ceilings being covered.

Foot painting

We have even done foot painting, with the floor covered in giant pieces of paper. But the mess in the loos put us off ever doing it again!

Stencils

Stencils made of paper or card can make painting more interesting. Try using stencils to produce posters, invitations, Christmas cards etc.

Spud printing

OK, they did it in Junior Church, but it could make a comeback. There are always swedes and carrots as well!

Blow painting

Pour a small quantity of fairly thin paint onto a sheet of paper and then, using a straw, blow the paint into patterns.

Stained glass painting

Make up pots of each of the colours you will need, including some black for the leading. Make the paint with powder paint and PVA glue. Using the mix, you will be able to paint onto polythene sheeting and produce your own stained glass windows. You could decorate the windows of the church hall at Christmas or Easter. The group could paint pictures that would communicate the Gospel to today's generation, as the stained glass windows of old did to previous generations.

Dry painting

Using PVA glue and a brush or spatula, draw shapes or patterns on paper, and then blow powder paint across it. The paint will stick to the glue. If this is done carefully, allowing time for drying, it is possible to use two or three different colours to create a really good effect.

We need to ask how the young people will learn through the task or the experience. For example, the murals should be based on a theme. It could be being a young person today, or it could be Jesus walking on the water. Even when the activity is great fun it also needs to have some teaching element to it.

Giant junk modelling

Junk modelling is a great activity. With ever-increasing numbers of recycling schemes being started, it is now possible to get good quality ingredients to use in addition to the loo rolls, yoghurt pots and egg boxes of *Blue Peter* fame.

The size of the junk creations you want to make will determine the number of people in each team. If you are using large cardboard tubes and wood to make frames for construction, you will need tools that are best used under supervision: saws, craft knives, hammers etc. So try to put an adult helper with each team.

As well as space rockets and underwater craft etc. there are a wide range of biblical junk constructions possible, e.g. Noah's Ark, Solomon's Temple, the walled city of Jericho, the Ark of the Covenant, the Tent of Meetings, an Egyptian pyramid etc.

Jewellery making

There are a number of suppliers who can provide the ingredients to make your own ear-rings, necklaces and bracelets. The cost of the materials is not that much, and large discounts can be obtained by bulk purchasing.

For ear-rings you will need: head-pins or eye-pins, ear-hooks or kidney wire, spacers, beads etc., fishing line or fuse wire. Practise assembling a pair yourself, and then let the members do it. Allow them to make extra pairs, but they will have to be paid for at cost price (usually well under £1).

For necklaces you will need: a screw-clasp with a loop or a bolt and jump-rings, an end bar, fishing line or cord, beads, spacers etc.

An evening of jewellery making does not have to be for girls only, though it will be in many groups. The lads may well enjoy the construction, even if they do not want to wear what they make.

Use as a discussion starter for a study of 1 Timothy 2:8–10.

Enamelling

Another popular activity. The young people can make jewellery, ornaments, badges etc. It can be either hot or cold enamelling.

Projection plays

You will need cut-out shapes, an overhead projector and a screen. The young people can write their own plays or dramatically retell Bible stories.

Mobiles

You will need stiff card, thin thread or fishing line, garden plant supports, scissors, pens, stencils, magazines (to copy outlines from), small nails and a hammer.

Wind chimes

These are noisy, heavier mobiles. Constructing them makes a really good youth group activity.

Candle making

This is a great activity. It must be its potential for mess that makes it so popular. You will need paraffin wax, cotton wicks, stearin (unless you buy wax with it already in), wax dyes and Vaseline (to prevent the candle sticking to the mould).

If you want to do it an alternative way, get everyone to bring along any old candles and pinch the bag of candle ends from church. Colour the different pans with a few chubby wax crayons from junior church.

Either way, you get a pan of hot wax ready to be poured into the mould. Use a variety of shapes, making sure that the candle can come out when it is set. Suspend the wick from a straw and tie the other end to a washer or similar metal object. Give your candle stripes by adding a colour, allowing it to cool, and then pouring on another colour.

Enormous badge making

A large circle/square/star of card and a pin, along with felt pens, paint and imagination can produce a giant badge. Making these badges can be a good activity for a new members' night, with each badge saying five things about the wearer. Or on a normal night, challenge the young people to produce the most amazing/large/psychedelic/edible etc. badge.

Banner making

Banners are a great way of decorating the youth group meeting-place, and they can be made cheaply and easily.

1. Draw or find a design that you would like on the banner and photocopy it. If it is over-complicated trace out the basic design in black. When you have the required design copy it on to an acetate sheet.

2. Take the sheet/piece of material etc. you are making the banner on and pin it to a wall. With an OHP project the image onto the sheet.

3. Draw round the outline in charcoal.

4. Take the banner down from the wall and place it on a plastic sheet to paint it. (Newspaper tends to stick, whereas a plastic sheet peels easily away and can be used many times.)

5. Paint the design on. Emulsion paint is the cheapest and easiest, but other kinds of paint tend to have better colours.
6. When the banner has been painted, carefully peel it off the plastic sheet (this is a two-person job) and hang it up to dry, making sure that it is not in contact with anything. You may need to put a clothes line up in the hall to peg it to.
7. After it has dried you can rivet the corners so that it can be tied to a pole and hung.

6

Talks

-TALKS-

Introduction

As a youth leader, Scout leader, curate or pastor the time will inevitably come when you are called upon to give a talk to a group of young people. Here are some tried and tested talks for young people that will work well in a variety of settings. When using them be bold and inventive, put in your own inflections and intonation and adapt them where necessary to suit the situation and the young people.

Some of the talks are borrowed, so a huge "Thank you" to the youth workers and clergy who lovingly produced the originals. Others have grown out of our ministry here at St Stephen's and with the Mushite Clan.

Ten tips for talks

1. Eye contact

You are talking to the young people, not to your notes or to the floor!

2. Be real

Be yourself. The young people will see through you if you are not being real with them, and then you can say goodbye to any respect.

3. Don't read it

Give the talk your own feelings, expression etc. and throw yourself into it!

4. Be dynamic

Use your voice and actions to really involve your audience. Make it easy for them to be involved. Show them you really mean it.

5. Be relevant

They will expect you not to be.

6. Be short

Their concentration will be limited. Once you have got them behind you they may listen for a bit longer.

7. Be fun

This is essential for talks and assemblies!

8. Where are the other two points?

Surprise and delight your audience by having fewer points to make than you threatened!

Pig stick

Topic covered

Our purpose in life is to have a relationship with God.

Equipment

A biro and some imagination.

Venue

A good talk for an assembly or for an evangelistic event.

Talk

Once upon a time, there was a ship sailing across a far and distant sea. When the winds blew strongly the sea turned into a boiling cauldron. The foaming waves beat against the boat, crashing over it and finally dashing it to pieces on the rocks. Everyone was killed apart from Jack who, being only small, had been tied to a spar. Jack was washed ashore by the tide onto a beautiful and lush desert island. Years went by and he grew strong on the wild fruit and vegetables.

One day, Jack was standing on a cliff top, staring over the ocean, when he saw a ship approaching the island. From the ship a small boat was rowed towards the shore. A man stepped out of the boat onto the beach. Jack stayed hidden in the undergrowth but continued to watch. The man jotted down a few things on a notepad, looked at the sand, returned to his boat and rowed away.

As he stepped into the boat Jack saw something fall onto the sand. What was it? What could it be? He waited for the boat to reach the ship and sail away and then he ran down to the beach [speaker runs up the aisle] and picked up the object [speaker brandishes a biro]. What was this strange object? What was it for?

As Jack investigated the object further, he discovered that it was made of two pieces [take the biro top off, put the top into a pocket and hold the biro as if it were a dagger]. "Ah ha!" said Jack, "it's a pig-stabber!" [rush forward into audience]. Jack chased, caught and stabbed a particularly

succulent-looking pig [pretend to grab and stab an appropriate member of the audience]. Jack dragged the pig back to his
camp-fire and threw it into his cooking pot [appropriate
actions].

So there was Jack, sitting watching the pot boil, stirring his
supper with his pig stabber [appropriate actions, and suck the
end of the biro to taste the brew]. Then he remembered the
other part of the mysterious object, still in his pocket [take
the top of the biro from the pocket]. What could this piece be
for? [Pick your ears, nose etc. and empty the imaginary
scrapings into the pot.] "Ah ha!" said Jack, "it's an ear-
picker." So, as he relaxed after eating a scrummy supper, Jack
had a pig-stabber, a pig stew-stirrer and an ear-picker.

What else could this object be for? He noticed that the little
blue piece at one end would in fact come out [take it out and
throw it away], and also that the pointed end would come out
too [remove this and keep it]. "Ah ha!" thought Jack to
himself, as he blew into the tube that remained [appropriate
actions]. He dashed over to a nearby spiny-dart bush to pick a
poison dart. Then he popped it into his new blow-pipe and ran
off to look for another, fatter pig [appropriate actions for
choosing a dart; creep down the aisle as if looking for a pig].
Spotting a really good pig, he took aim and blew [appropriate
action and noises] down the pipe . . . success! Jack smiled to
himself as he dragged his new catch back to his cooking pot.

Comment

So Jack had found four uses for his pig stick:

1. A pig-stabber
2. A pig stew-stirrer
3. An ear-picker
4. A blow-pipe

All good uses, but not one of them was the one that it was
created for. [Hold up the biro.] What was it created for? [Ask

the audience.] For writing! It had a purpose.

The same is true of your life. You can find all sorts of uses for your life: making money, doing good, chasing this, seeking after that . . . but unless you find the purpose for which you are created, you are as much use as a pig-stabber.

God says we are created to have an eternal, dynamic relationship with Him. If we are not in that relationship with God, we are missing the whole purpose of being alive.

Ending

Finish with an appropriate ending. E.g.:

1. An evangelistic challenge.
2. An opportunity for repentance and recommitment.
3. A quiet prayer or pause for thought.

Slime

Topic covered

Redemption and salvation.

Equipment

One Slime Jar (an empty glass sweet jar etc.), five £1 coins, a towel, a bowl of water, some paper towel.

Venue

This is a great talk for a youth service, a school assembly or a youth group meeting.

Ingredients for the Slime Jar

Place into the Jar the following:

half a pint of washing-up liquid
one pint of water
three used tea-bags
cold spaghetti (cooked or uncooked)
baked beans
red food colouring
macaroni

Add any other bits and pieces to make the mixture look and feel as revolting as possible.

Talk

Who would like £1? [Ask the audience. When someone says yes, ask them to come to the front and get it. Give that person the £1. Ask the audience the same question once more whilst holding out a £1 coin. Invite one person up to the front and then drop the coin into the Slime Jar. Tell the volunteer that if he/she puts his/her hand into the Jar and rescues the coin, it will be his/hers. Whilst this is being done you can ask questions like:]

What does it feel like? Have you got the coin? Is anything moving about in there? What does it smell like? Can you feel the veins? [Wait for the horrified "Agggrrhhh!" from the audience.]

[When the volunteer has the coin tell him/her to rinse and dry his/her hands. Ask for more volunteers, using appropriate comments each time to give the whole thing a fun feel. When all the coins have been retrieved talk to the group on any of the points below:]

1. We live in sin, and only if we are taken out of the slime into which we have fallen can we be cleansed and returned to our rightful place.

2. God was prepared to get involved in the sin of the world to rescue us.

3. Despite the slime, the £1 coin was worth rescuing. To God we are so valuable that we are worth rescuing.

4. Other points on the salvation of man as appropriate to your situation.

Puddles

Topic covered

Guidance/our relationship with God.

Equipment

15 paper puddle shapes, about 50cm × 75cm, cut out of newspaper. An airhorn, a blindfold and an assistant.

Venue

A youth group of any size, a church service, a Christian Union meeting or a Scout/Guide group.

Talk

Hello, it's good to be here. [Introduce yourself and your assistant, who will be playing God.]

[Ask a volunteer to come out to the front. Blindfold him/her and make sure that he/she cannot see. While you are blindfolding the volunteer, have your assistant arrange the paper puddles in the aisle. Spin the volunteer so that their sense of direction is confused, and then tell them that they have to walk to God (who needs to keep quiet). Stand God at one end of the line of puddles and the blindfolded volunteer at the other end.]

[If the volunteer manages to head off in a Godward direction he/she will inevitably tread on a puddle. Whenever they do, give a blast on the airhorn. After several blasts, or if the person gets to God, let your assistant bring them back.]

[Ask for a second volunteer and repeat the exercise. This time God may yell helpful guiding comments from his end of the hall or aisle. There should be fewer blasts on the airhorn.]

[Repeat again with a third volunteer, but this time, after they have been blindfolded, have God come down and take them by the hand and lead them through the puddles without stepping on any.]

People sometimes imagine that God is rather like our first illustration. He stands far away in heaven and leaves us to get on with it, and we just stumble through life, falling into one difficult situation after another.

Other people think God is like illustration number two. He stands in heaven yelling instructions to us. Sometimes we follow these and so avoid the pitfalls, while at other times we go astray and end up in a mess.

God is really like illustration number three. He is our loving heavenly Father who wants to take us by the hand and guide us. When we become a Christian we begin a personal relationship with God. He is always there to guide and help us, to give us strength and encouragement. All that we have to do to begin that relationship is to become a Christian.

[End with an evangelistic challenge or an opportunity for recommitment etc.]

Mars Bars

Topic covered

Popular excuses for not standing up for the Christian faith at school.

Venue

A school assembly, a youth group or youth service.

Equipment

Two £1 coins, two Mars Bars.

Talk

Have you noticed how many of the TV game shows are giving out free money? Well, anything they can do we can do, so who would like £1? [Watch for the first hand to go up and throw the person a £1 coin.] Would anybody else like some free money? [Throw another £1 coin.] Sorry, there's no more free money, but does anybody want a Mars Bar? [When two hands go up ask them out to the front.]

Hello. You are . . .? John.

And you are . . .? Jill.

It's really good of you to come up here like this! Did either of you have breakfast? [Whatever their answer is:] I expect you're hungry, so what I'd like you both to do is just to stand here and slowly eat your Mars Bar, so that everyone can see how much you're enjoying it. [As the two eat the Mars Bars you need to keep up a stream of comments to put them off and to get the non-participants participating. Comments such as:]

How are you feeling? Do you feel self-conscious up here in front of 500 people?

By the way, there's a bit stuck on your chin.

Do you feel thirsty?

Mars Bars can give you indigestion.

In one school where I was doing this assembly, someone choked to death.

I was going to buy some Mars Bars, but then I found these two down the back of the fridge.

[And then, when they have finished eating:] How did it feel, doing something no one else was doing in front of so many people? [Let them answer.]

[Then to the audience:] Let's give Jill and John a round of applause as they go back to their seats.

You're probably wondering what this is all about, and that's a really good question. Some of you will be really shocked to see Mars Bars being eaten openly on stage. In most places all Mars Bar-eaters gather secretly so that no one will know what they are up to.

For those of you who don't eat Mars Bars, there seem to be a number of reasons:

1. None of my friends eat Mars Bars, so I don't.
2. My parents didn't eat Mars Bars, so I grew up without eating them and have never thought about eating them.
3. It isn't trendy to eat Mars Bars today. Everyone's into Secrets or Twirls. I wouldn't want to be out of fashion.
4. Mars Bars are a crutch. You should be able to get by in life without them.
5. Mars Bars are for children. You'll grow out of them – wait and see.
6. I know all about Mars Bars: how and where they are made, and what the price is. Why do I need to eat one?

Whether you are a secret Mars Bar eater or whether you've never eaten a Mars Bar, the fact of the matter is that if it's true that a Mars a day helps you work, rest and play, then you should tell everyone, and never mind the excuses. The parallel is quite clear: if we know that Jesus Christ died and rose again, we should tell it to people too.

Hints

All the above excuses are parallel to the excuses given for avoiding Christianity. You may feel it right to talk on some of these or not. Adjust the talk as appropriate.

The talk has actually been done without mentioning Jesus at all. The response was amazing, as people discussed what the talk meant. The Christian Union then had a great opportunity to witness.

Prayer

Equipment

An umbrella and some scrap sheets of paper.

Venue

A youth service, a youth group talk etc.

Talk

One of the things that I've noticed is how often the service sheets get converted into paper aeroplanes. So rather than waiting for you guys to get bored near the end of the talk, I thought that this week you could make the aeroplanes at the beginning. Don't worry if you haven't got any paper, because I've brought some along. [Pass out the paper to those who want it. Fetch the umbrella and open it up. Place it upside down on the floor at the front. Give them time to finish making their aeroplanes.] On the command "Go!" everyone is to throw their paper aeroplanes from where they are sitting into the umbrella. [Have a bag of prizes for those who succeed.]

Sometimes we imagine that prayer is rather like lobbing our requests into God's umbrella. Almost all of them go astray, but a few reach the target. Whenever we fail that exam or we don't get the birthday present we wanted or we feel ignored by our friends, we feel that our "aero-prayers" have missed their mark.

So if that's what prayer is not like, what is prayer actually like?

1. God always hears our prayers. But He can answer them in one of three ways: "Yes", "No" or "Wait". Sometimes our prayers are based on purely selfish motives. At other times, prayers can be a substitute for action. At other times

our prayers come from the pain and anguish we are experiencing in our lives. God's answer takes into consideration the situations that we are in and the feelings and motives that we have.

2. God loves us and wants only what is best for us. This is not necessarily the same thing as giving us what we want.

3. Prayer is about a relationship: talking to God and listening to Him. If you had a friend whose only conversation with you was "I want this" and "Can I have this?" you would soon get very bored of them. God never gets bored of us, but He must sometimes find the conversation a little bit limiting! We need to listen to God as well as talk to Him.

4. Prayer is about change. As our relationship with God develops, we will find ourselves being changed, and so our prayers will change and develop. We will become less concerned with ourselves and more concerned with doing God's will.

These days we tend to hear a lot about balanced diets and healthy eating. Similarly, we need to have a balanced "prayer diet" if we are to pray in a healthy way. The five ingredients of a healthy prayer life are:

1. Praise God for who He is.
2. Admit to God all that you have done wrong.
3. Thank God for His forgiveness and all that He's done.
4. Hear God speaking to you through the Bible and through your times of prayer.
5. State your needs, anxieties and concerns.

Now let's pray.

The Holy Spirit

Topic covered

Being filled with the Holy Spirit, and the gifts of the Spirit.

Equipment

A large, deep waterproof tray, a jug of water, three plastic cups (one of which should have holes in the bottom and another of which should have some dirt in it), a ping-pong ball, a circle of card.

Venue

A church youth group, a church weekend away, an ordinary service . . .

Talk

One of the most difficult things to understand in the Christian life is the Holy Spirit. Today we hope not only to understand more about Him but also to experience more of Him.

Image that you are like this cup [hold the cup upside down over the tray]. God's Holy Spirit is like the water. He surrounds us and challenges us but He does not dwell in us. God has given us free will, and unless we freely open ourselves to the Holy Spirit, He will not barge His way in. The Bible says that when we become a Christian we become a new creation. We completely change the direction our life is going in. This is rather like turning the cup the right way up [pour some water into the cup]. Now God's Spirit is not only all around us, but He is also inside us. As Paul says in Ephesians, we have been marked with a seal, the promised Holy Spirit, so we are like the cup, full of the refreshing goodness of God. Often after we have become a Christian that is what it is like: we love to pray, we read our Bibles a lot and we enjoy worshipping God. But then, over a period of time, we find that it gets harder. There are three reasons for this:

1. We leak [pick up the cup with holes in and pour water into it]. Because we are living in a fallen world the Holy Spirit

leaks out of us. So unless you keep well stocked up you'll run dry.
2. We cut off the supply. When we sin and turn away from God, in effect we are putting a lid on our lives and excluding God [demonstrate trying to pour the water in with the card over the top of the cup]. God is still the abundant Giver – He hasn't changed. It is us who are closed to Him.
3. There may be areas of our lives we don't want God to be Lord of [pick up the cup with the soil in it]. If we are like the cup with the soil in it we are not overflowing with the goodness of God but with a confusing mixture. We get disheartened and disappointed that we are not living up to God's standards, and we can get trapped into trying hard to do the right things rather than relying on *God*.

What are the solutions if we are in these situations?

1. We need to be constantly being filled with the Holy Spirit. It is not a one-off experience but an everyday one. In your daily times of prayer and Bible study ask God to fill you with His Spirit.
2. If you have sinned, don't forget to confess it. Say to God, "I'm sorry, I've blown it again." Do you know the good news? God will forgive us! He doesn't say, "That's the tenth time you've done that – I'm not going to forgive you!" He really forgives.
3. If there are areas you don't want God to know about, the truth is that He already does know. He knows every hair on your head. He knew you in the womb, he knows your every thought. But not only does He know all this, but He loves you as well. So you can trust Him completely: He's the one person who always wants the best for you. If you do trust Him, then you'll be open to all that He has to pour in, and you will overflow with the goodness of God.

[You could end the talk here, but if you want to take the matter further, here are some more ideas:]

If you are a Christian, God can use you to minister in the power of the Holy Spirit. It doesn't matter how young or how old you are. He doesn't use you because you are famous or because you know all about the Bible; rather, He will use you because you have made yourself available to Him.

Let's imagine that God has a prophetic message for someone. We'll use this ping-pong ball to represent the message [place the ball in the jug]. (Of course, the same lesson applies to any of the other gifts of the Spirit, like healing, a word of knowledge etc.) What would happen if this gift were to be given to a person who is cut off from God by sin? They cannot receive the gift [demonstrate with the jug and cup]. If the gift is given to a person with areas closed off by sin they may or may not receive the gift, but it may become mixed with the mud and be confused if they do receive it. If the gift is given to a person open to God, they will be able to receive and use it [continue to pour water into the cup so that it overflows].

Sometimes God will give us the same gift several times. He may use us often in prayer for healing, or it may be a one-off gift. [You could make the distinction here between a gift and a ministry, a ministry being the long-term use of a gift. But if your young people are new to ministering in the power of the Holy Spirit, leave this issue for later.]

The only requirement to be used by God is being open. Let's have a time of openness to the Holy Spirit. We don't have to sing lots of songs, we don't need to be emotional, we just need to want to receive from God.

Let's all stand [give everyone time to stretch and be comfortable].

We want to receive from God, so we may find it helpful to hold our hands open in front of us, as if we were going to receive a material gift.

I'm going to say a prayer, and then we will be quiet and still, waiting on God.

[Pray a prayer inviting God's Holy Spirit to move, then be still and wait. Don't be frightened by the silence; allow the

Spirit plenty of time. Remember that it is God you are waiting on, so you don't have to panic.]

[When you feel it is right, give thanks in a prayer and sing a quiet worship song.]

[Ask if any of the young people would like to share what they experienced. This may include things like:

peace
tears
a deeper experience of Jesus' sacrifice for us
pictures or prophetic visions
shaking and trembling
a great joy and laughter
the gift of tongues
a feeling of being cleansed
a call from God to do something

These are some of the experiences which young people under 15 have had when we have had times of being open to the Holy Spirit. Your experiences may be very different, but God is totally trustworthy.]

[After those who want to have shared their experiences, end with a song of joy and praise.]

How much are you worth?

Topic covered

How valuable we are to God.

Equipment

A mystery prize wrapped up in wrapping paper.

Venue

A school assembly, a youth group talk, a service etc.

Talk

Who would like to have the opportunity to win the contents of this mystery box? [Ask the first three people with their hands up to come out to the front. Ask them their names and introduce them to the audience.]

I am going to ask each of you three questions. The contestant who gets the most questions correct will win the mystery prize. The contestant who gets the least questions correct will collect a special prize.

Contestant 1:
1. Where were you born?
2. How many animals did Noah take on board the ark?
3. What is the value of the mystery box?

Contestant 2:
1. Where were you born?
2. What was Adam's wife called?
3. What is the value of the mystery box?

Contestant 3:
1. Where were you born?
2. Who was the third king after Jeroboam?
3. Spell "Mephibosheth" backwards.

[If there is a tie, ask a tie-breaker question, e.g. "Name a disciple." When you have a winner, give him/her the mystery prize and allow him/her to open it and then return to his/her seat. Send the second-place contestant back to his/her place also, and then address the loser.]

Well, as you know, times are hard and the youth budget has been the victim of the recession . . . so to raise the funds to give away such fantastic mystery prizes, I have decided that we are going to sell the loser. I hope you don't mind, but it's tough if you do!

[Stand the loser on a chair so that all the audience may view the "merchandise". Check the teeth, feel the muscles etc. Ask the audience:]

What am I bid? [As the bids come in, ask people to hold the money in the air. This keeps the bids low.] There is an alternative, if you lot don't want to buy him/her. I know a local chemist who will quite happily supply the constituent chemicals at a reasonable price. Now let's see just what we have. [Turn and look at the person on the chair, as if that will give you a clue.]

Enough water here to fill a ten-gallon barrel, but it's not exactly Perrier. Enough fat for seven bars of soap. Enough carbon for 9,000 pencils. (Maybe the art teachers will want to make a bid now?) Enough phosphorus for 2,200 match-heads. Enough iron for a medium-sized nail. Enough lime to white-wash an outside loo. A small quantity of magnesium and enough sulphur to de-worm a dog.

Right, I make that about £10. Hands up if you think that's all that X is worth. But the Bible says that he/she is worth much more than that. The Bible says that we are not the chance products of a meaningless universe – we are not just a jumble of chemicals. Actually, we are created in the image of God. We have a purpose and a destiny. Our worth has been demon-strated by the fact that God sent His only Son, Jesus, to die on the cross for us and to enable us to fulfil our purpose and destiny. So, the next time someone asks you what you are worth, remember that you are so special that the God of the universe was willing to die for you.

Let's pray.

Dettox removes doubt

Topic covered

Trusting in Jesus.

Equipment

A bottle of Dettox spray surface cleaner (or a similar product) with the Dettox replaced with water (you will need to thoroughly wash the inside out and squirt plenty of warm water through the nozel), five hard-boiled eggs and two chairs.

Venue

A school assembly, a youth service, a youth group evening etc.

Talk

It's great to be here, and I need a few volunteers. Three will do. [Choose the first three to put their hands up and ask them to come out to the front. Ask them their names and introduce them to the audience.]

Who wants to go first? [When one volunteers ask the other two to step to one side.]

What I would like you to do is to juggle these three eggs – they are all hard-boiled. Do you believe you can do that? [If he/she succeeds, continue adding eggs until he/she doesn't believe he/she can juggle that number. Then ask him/her to stand to one side.]

[Bring back to the centre of the stage volunteer number two.] Your task is much easier. What I would like you to do is to stand on this chair and, without touching the floor, get yourself to that chair over there. [Point to another chair which is too far away to jump to. The volunteer is not allowed to move the chairs from their present positions. When he/she decides that it is too hard, ask him/her to stand with the first volunteer at the side.]

Now it's the third volunteer's turn. What I would like you to do is to float six inches off the ground while doing an impression of Jason Donovan being eaten by piranhas. [Let him/her try for a minute.] Well, I'm not sure about the impression, but you didn't manage the floating off the ground. Don't worry – I have the solution in this bag. If all three of you line up here, I'll get the solution out. [Go and fetch the Dettox spray from the bag.] The label on this bottle says that this spray removes doubt, so what I'm going to do is spray you with it. Then you'll all believe and be able to do your tasks. [Spray each one with the water, asking the audience if they think that the volunteers have been sprayed enough to remove their doubt.]

[Bring back volunteer one and see if he/she can now juggle. Really hype the audience. Bring back volunteer two and see if he/she can leap the gap. Bring back volunteer three and see if he/she can float.]

[Thank volunteer one and let him/her return to his/her seat with a small prize.] What would volunteer one need to be a juggler? Practice, training etc.

How can volunteer two get from this chair to the other? No, it's not impossible. He/she just needs help to be able to do it. [Carry him/her across to the other chair, then thank him/her and give a small prize.]

How can volunteer three float? If the laws of gravity changed it could be possible. [Thank him/her and give a prize.] Let's have a round of applause for our volunteers!

There are three quick points about the Christian faith which we can learn from this:

1. There are some things in the Christian life we have to work at, like doing our Bible study or praying. Simply trying to overcome our doubts often doesn't help, whereas training and practice will.
2. In some things in the Christian life we need the support of our fellow Christians: we need their help to cope with our hurts, disappointments etc. These things don't go away if we just try to believe that everything is all OK. We need to share honestly with others and receive prayer, healing and support.
3. Some things in the Christian life seem impossible if we don't recognize that God is outside of time and space and is

the Creator of everything. Because of this He can intervene in miraculous and amazing ways. As we walk with God and experience Him in our everyday life, our doubts recede and we can be more certain of the amazing things God has done.

So, do we need an anti-doubt spray? No! The best solution to doubt is to trust God.

The unknown chocolate bar

Topic covered

Pre-evangelistic talk to non-Christians.

Equipment

Two or three chocolate bars from overseas that the young people will not recognize (the more similar they are to something on sale in this country the better). You may be able to find something suitable at Marks and Spencer's or at an up-market sweet shop.

Venue

A Scout Camp, a Sunday service, a youth group etc.

Talk

Turn to the person next to you and tell them they are a beautiful human being. They have to reply, "Thank you, so are you."

Now face to the left, place your hands on the shoulders of the person in front and gently massage their shoulders. Now turn the other way and massage the ankles of the person in front.

We need three volunteer couples out the front. [Play the Cotton bud Game (see Chapter 7).]

Who would like to eat a chocolate bar? [Ask two or three volunteers to come up on stage and give them an already unwrapped chocolate bar so that they cannot see the label. Now tell the volunteers:] Take a good look at the bar. Smell it. What colour is it? Now take a bite. What does it taste of? What colour is the inside? [When they have eaten it ask them to guess what it is. When they guess incorrectly ask the audience/congregation if they can guess. Talk about some of the reasons why it was not easy to guess:]

1. It wasn't like we expected it to be. It looked like one thing on the outside but was different on the inside.
2. We didn't have the wrapper that would have identified it.
3. We had never seen it before.

[Dig out a wrapper to show people what the sweets are and where you got them from.]

We can say the same things about Christianity as we did about the bar:

1. If we have never experienced Christianity before we won't know what it is like.
2. We don't have enough information about Christianity – it's like not having the chocolate bar wrapper. Many of us have never been to a living church, read our Bibles or found out for ourselves what Christianity is all about.
3. We think we know what Christianity is like, but really we don't. Young people often think Christianity is about a long list of do's and don'ts and rights and wrongs, but actually it is primarily concerned with a personal relationship with God through Jesus.

If we want to know what a chocolate bar is really like, we need to try it. Exactly the same is true for Christianity: only if we are a Christian can we know for ourselves what it is like.

[Close with an opportunity for people to become Christians or to get a leaflet explaining how they can.]

7

Games & Wacky Ideas

Introduction
Strobe Football
Guzzle
Twin Coke Drinking
Baby Photos
Spaghetti Numbers
The World's Largest . . .
The Chair Race
Crazy Mixer
People Awards
Giant Human Board Games
Cotton Bud Game
Affirmation Candles
Dear Thomas
Cooking

Icing Prayers
Kingdom Meals
Healthy Choice
Donuts
Overhead Feeding
Chopstick M & M
Youth Group Exchange
Caption Competition
Colour Clash
Human Dominoes
Overhead Notices
Record, Tape & Book
  Library
Telephone Care Share
Prayer Breakfasts

-GAMES-
+WACKY IDEAS

Maxine sensed they wanted her to volunteer

Introduction

There are some people who do not like games in their youth group programme, and there are others who only have games and fun activities. I have placed this chapter near to the back of this book partly because our young people need a balanced diet of activities. A programme consisting entirely of games and fun activities will produce the "Roundabout" phenomenon (as mentioned in Chapter 1), and that is a situation which will produce very little or no spiritual growth. However, it is great occasionally to have fun games just for the fun of it. Here is a selection of wacky ideas that I have picked up over the last year.

Strobe football

Aim

Absolutely none. If you find one, please write to tell me!

Equipment

Two strobe lights, a sorbo sponge football and a dark hall.

Hints

This game is best played on dark, wet winter nights. If you have members of your group who are epileptic or who find that strobe lights make them feel ill, avoid this game, as it's

not fair to make them sit in the kitchen while everyone else
has fun.

How to play

1. Choose two teams by some appropriate means. It may help
if there are the same number in each team.
2. Send them to either end of the hall to get acquainted, plan
tactics etc.
3. Play the game like normal football for two minutes, and
then switch the lights off and use the strobes for one twenty-
second burst every minute.
4. Watch the chaos and keep score.

Guzzle

Aim

Thirst-quenching fun.

Equipment

One straw per player, one bucketful of soft drink per team.

Preparation

Wash the buckets out thoroughly and make up the soft drink.

How to play

Divide the group into teams. On the command "Go!" they
can start drinking. The team that finishes their bucket first is
the winner.

Twin Coke-drinking competition

Aim

A fun up-front game.

Equipment

Two bottles of Coca-Cola (the traditional type) per contestant and some masking tape.

Preparation

Tape each contestant's two bottles together around the widest part.

Action

Open the bottles and give them to the contestants. On the command "Go!" they have to drink the contents of both the bottles, spilling as little as possible and not separating the two bottles. The winner is the first to successfully complete the task.

Baby photos

Aim

A fun mixer.

Equipment

Paper, pencils, photo-mounting corners and a marker pen.

Preparation

A couple of weeks before the event ask all the group members to find a photo of themselves when they were a baby. They must not show them to the rest of the group. Mount these on pieces of paper and mark them (a), (b), (c) etc.

How to play

On the evening put all the photos up round the room and give everyone a piece of paper and a pencil. They need to write down the letters and next to them put who they think the photo is of. When everyone is finished, in turn people own up to whose photo is whose. Give a prize to the person who correctly identified the most photos.

Spaghetti numbers

Aim

Fun and team building.

Equipment

Per team: a bowl of spaghetti numbers, a piece of sugar-paper numbered 1 to 10 down the side, paper towels (optional), an old telephone directory and a list of ten people and/or organizations.

Action

Divide the group up into teams of four. The task is to find the telephone numbers of the people/organizations by looking them up in the directory (it can be good to include numbers it might be useful for the young people to know, e.g. the youth leaders, the local police, the minister, Childline etc.) and to write them out in spaghetti on the sugar-paper next to the corresponding number. The first team to satisfactorily complete the task is the winner.

Hints

You will need to clean up afterwards, as the easiest way to find the spaghetti numbers is to spread them across the table.

The world's largest

Create a wacky youth group challenge to make the world's largest something. One group we heard of were particularly piggy and made the world's largest ice-cream sundae, using a seven-foot length of guttering, gallons of ice-cream and all the trimmings.

Giant food things are great fun to do (and to eat!), but we do live in a world where two thirds of the people go to bed hungry. Many of them are our brothers and sisters in Christ. We need to be careful to live out a biblical and balanced approach.

Instead of food, go for the world's largest heap of litter picked/home-grown runner bean/penny mile etc., or the most people to meet in a loo, or the highest Bible study above sea level, or the strangest place to read Genesis etc. The stranger and more way-out the challenge, the better.

The chair race

Aim

Team building.

Equipment

Five chairs per team.

How to play

Divide the group into teams of six. Line the teams up behind a start line at one end of the hall, with their stack of five chairs behind them.

Mark off a finishing line at the other end of the hall.

Each team have to transport themselves and all the chairs from one end of the hall to the other without stepping on the floor between the start and finish lines. The chairs must not be moved by sliding, they can only be lifted and then placed. If a player touches the floor, he/she must return to the beginning.

The first team to have all its chairs stacked and to get all its members across the finish line wins.

Crazy mixer

Aim

A start-of-term mixer – a fun activity for when new members join.

Equipment

A pencil and a Crazy Mixer Sheet for each person.

CRAZY MIXER SHEET

1. Get five people to write their names out in full (including any really embarrassing middle names!) on the back of this sheet.
2. Unlace somebody's shoe.
3. Leapfrog over somebody five times.
4. Get a hair from someone's head (let them remove it!).
5. Get someone to do a somersault.
6. Get someone of the opposite gender to do five press-ups.
7. Sing the National Anthem to someone.
8. Play "Ring a ring of roses" with someone (out loud!).
9. Find someone who has the same number of letters in their first name as you and arm-wrestle them.
10. Change an item of clothing with someone.

The winner is the first person to complete all the tasks.

People awards

Hold an annual award ceremony for the youth group. This could be done on a week/weekend away, but it would be more fun if done on a special evening.

Invite a number of "celebrities" (i.e. those who have "starred" over the year at different youth group events, e.g. leaders, helpers, speakers, friendly adults etc.) to come to the event to give out the awards.

Design the awards so that everybody gets one. These might include awards for: always helping with the washing up; always being punctual; always being late; getting totally covered in mud at the "It's a Knockout" etc. The awards themselves should be home-made certificates.

On the night lay out the tables and chairs like at an Oscar ceremony.

As you read out the nominations, include the names of some well-known stars from the pop and film world. Let each person make an acceptance speech.

Through the evening the leaders could serve non-alcoholic cocktails to create an atmosphere. Have an interval for a band or other entertainment.

The whole purpose of the exercise is to affirm the young people and to make them feel wanted and included.

Giant human board games

Instead of playing a little board game, why not have a human-sized variant? People are the pieces and the whole hall is the board. Squares may be marked off with masking tape, and a giant dice can be made out of cardboard. The opposing teams have to move people instead of counters or pieces. Find any game that the young people are into and adapt it accordingly.

The Cotton bud game

Aim

An up-front mixer.

Equipment

One box of cotton buds.

How to play

Ask three or four mixed couples out to the front. It doesn't matter if they don't know each other – that's half the fun.

Give each of the guys eight cotton buds. Their task is to place them in their facial orifices (mouth, ears and nose). They are not allowed to put more than two in any one place.

When they have done this, the real fun starts, because the girls' job is to remove the cotton buds, one at a time, using only their teeth. The first pair to have removed all the cotton buds are the winners.

Affirmation candles

Aim

Group building and personal affirmation.

Equipment

One candle per person, one large candle, one cross.

Preparation

Create a mellow atmosphere – e.g. a quiet worship tape and subdued lighting. Arrange the seats in a semi-circle around the lighted candle and the cross.

Action

1. As people arrive, give them an unlit candle and ask them to sit quietly on a chair.
2. When everyone is gathered, turn the lights and the music off and let everyone enjoy the quiet.
3. Explain to the group that we are going to use this time to affirm one another. One person will go forward and light his/her candle from the one by the cross. Then, going to another person, he/she will say, "I'm really glad you are a member of this group because . . ." Then they will light that person's candle with their own. They then blow out their own candle and return to their seat.
4. A third person can then go and light their candle from the one by the cross and do the same. The second person goes and says to someone why they appreciate them being in the group, and then lights their candle, and so on. If a person's candle has been lit by someone else they do not blow it out after affirming someone.
5. The exercise will slowly build up, but try to stop the young people becoming slight in their comments. Make sure that everyone is included.
6. When everyone has a lighted candle, have a few moments of quiet and a prayer.
7. Blow out the candles and put on the low lights. Let people share what they felt and also any lessons they can draw out from it.
8. Finish with a quiet chat, or move on to something completely different.

Dear Thomas

Aim

To provide a mechanism for the members to raise any questions or doubts in an anonymous way.

Equipment

A box with a letter slot in it (decorated and labelled appropriately), some pens and some paper or cards.

Action

Introduce Thomas the Letterbox to the group. Say that any letters going to him do not have to be signed, and that any questions asked will be answered during future group meetings in a way that will encourage the young people to be open and honest about their faith.

As letters come in, do not use them as a way of working out who is thinking or worrying about what, and don't approach those who have written the letters, even if they do put their names on them. Create opportunities for them to talk to you. This will encourage more of the young people to ask real questions.

If you get a question you cannot answer, be honest and tell the group you don't know. For some questions, your pastor may be able to provide an answer. For others, there may not be an answer, only conjecture, so say so.

All the answers should build up the young people's faith and give them the knowledge to articulate their faith to their friends.

Cooking

This is a favourite youth group activity, even amongst the boys. As well as the large projects like a parents' meal or a strawberry tea and the food socials (see elsewhere in this book), it is possible to use cooking on an ordinary evening.

Icing prayers

You will need: icing sugar, food colouring, cake mix (packeted caterers' mix from a cash and carry), cake-tins of assorted shapes and sizes, grease-proof paper and scissors.

While some of the members are making up the cake mix, others will be greasing the tins. The cooking may well have to be done on a rota, as the oven will only be able to take so many cakes at a time.

While they are cooking, people need to write some prayers, choosing topics relevant to young people today.

By the time they have done this, the first cakes will be ready to come out. If your group is quick or if the cakes take a long time, use the spare minutes for some teaching on prayer.

While the cakes are cooling, the icing needs to be made and the icing writing cones need to be made from the grease-proof paper. Make several bowls of icing, each a different colour.

Everyone then has to ice their cake with their prayer in whatever form, style or colour combination they want.

When everyone has finished, admire the handywork, pray a couple of the prayers and eat the cakes. Sell off the remaining ones at church on Sunday for youth group funds.

Kingdom meals

These can be anything from chips and cola to Chinese cuisine. The important thing is not what you eat, but how you eat it. No one is allowed to feed themselves or to serve themselves, and there is to be no reciprocal feeding, i.e. you cannot feed the person who is feeding you.

The setting and style can greatly add to the effect, and, of course, it's much more fun if the group have cooked the meal themselves rather than gone down the take-away.

Healthy choice

Hold a fun food evening. Divide the group into teams, each of which has to prepare one course for a meal. A local food nutritionist or dietitian can then say what's good or bad about it. This could lead into a discussion of what it means for the body to be the temple of the Holy Spirit.

Donuts

When the nights are long and youth group meeting finishes in the rain and snow, there is nothing better than home-made donuts with hot chocolate to end the evening.

Overhead feeding

Two players lie on their backs so that the tops of their heads are touching. They both have a jar of baby food and a spoon. The object is to feed the other as much of the jar as you can. This can be played as a cooperative game or as a competition between two or more pairs. It's gross!

Chopstick M & M

Three players come out to the front and the winner is the first to eat a bowl of M & M's. The only difficulty is that the competitors have to use chopsticks to do it!

Youth group exchange

Why not twin your youth group with another group from a very different part of the country? If you are a city group, team up with a rural one; if you are a suburban group, get together with one from an inner city area. You could even (dare I suggest it?) cross denominational and churchmanship boundaries!

Caption competition

One way of making young people feel that they belong and that they are wanted is to take photos or video film of them.

It's always good to put up the latest batch on the notice board. But just for a change, why not run a caption competition? The young people can write humorous suggestions for what was being said at the time the photos were taken.

Colour clash

Everyone has to choose their favourite colour. They then find someone whose favourite colour is different, and then each person tries to persuade the other to change to their own favourite colour. (See *Youthbuilders* for the game in full.) The game leads on into Human Dominoes.

Human dominoes

Each pair of people with their favourite colours is to act like a domino. The task for the group is to link all the pairs together to form a continuous line. You may need to help by saying scarlet is the same as red etc., but otherwise leave the group to see if they can do it without cheating.

Overhead notices

Instead of the usual reading of the notices, why not write them up onto acetate and use the overhead projector to project them on the ceiling? Everyone has to lie on their backs to read them.

Record, tape and book library

Why not set up a library of Christian records, tapes and books? Older Christian young people may well have unwanted books etc. from when they were aged eleven to fourteen. Add to the library by giving the young people a certain amount to spend every other month from youth group funds and letting them choose what to get.

Telephone care share

Why not ring up the young people in the youth group, not because you want them to do something or because you want to remind them of an event, but just to see how they are and to let them know that you are remembering them in your prayers?

Prayer breakfasts

These are great fun. We recently held a youth group meeting before school on a Friday, and the young people brought friends to it! The agenda is usually food first (a full cooked breakfast), then share concerns, then pray about them. Even if the young people are too shy to pray out loud at first, they will in time develop enough confidence to do so.

8

Outdoor Activities

Introduction

Scavenger Hunts

Scavenger Hunt 1
TNT Scavenger Hunt
Survival Scavenger Hunt

Bike Rodeo

Slalam Race Relay
Sudden Death Sprints
No Hands Trial
Bike Hurdles
Balloon Mace Massacre
Ball in Bucket

It's a Knockout

Blindfold Course
Tyre Race
Wet Wellies
Box Towers
Relay Madness

Team Challenges

Egg Launch
Electric Fence
Arrows
Blind Numbers
Crate Crush

Backwoods Evening

OUTDOOR ACTIVITIES

INTRODUCTION

Young people aged eleven to fourteen really enjoy outdoor activities and challenges. As well as being great fun, they can also provide mental and physical stimulation and team-building opportunities. The summer is obviously the best time for outdoor activities, with the light evenings, but it's good to try to keep a balance – don't completely omit teaching and other indoor activities. Also, an outdoor activity in the winter months can make a really good variation to the programme. Before organizing any activity that is likely to involve a risk (and even a night hike has that), make sure that you are adequately covered by insurance.

SCAVENGER HUNTS

Scavenger hunt 1

Aim

To get the group working cooperatively in teams to complete the greatest number of tasks in a given time.

Equipment

Per team: a copy of the sheet below (adapted if necessary to suit your group), a pencil (and if you decide to use the tasks as below:) a wax crayon, a plastic rubbish sack, a sheet of paper and a plastic/paper cup.

Scavenger hunt task sheet

You have 60 minutes to complete as many tasks as possible. For each task where a signature is needed a space is provided. You may do the tasks in any order. NB there are different point scores for each task. The members of your group must stay together.

Task 1
Obtain a wax crayon rubbing of a policeman/woman's cap-badge on the paper provided (25 points).

Policeman/woman's signature: ....

Task 2
Visit the Chinese takeaway and obtain a menu signed by the person serving and all the customers (15 points).

Task 3
Obtain one of today's newspapers (10 points).

Task 4
Find a complete stranger who is willing to sign your feet and then sign here as well (20 points):

....

Task 5
Go and sing a full Christmas carol at the vicarage (15 points).

Signed: ....

Task 6
Find a stranger who will do a handstand for you, and get them to sign here (10 points):

....

Task 7
Visit the Methodist Youth Group and offer to be their slaves for five minutes (15 points).

Methodist Youth Leader to sign here: ....

Task 8
Collect as many soft drink cans as you can find and bring them back with you (1 point for every different can).

Task 9
Find out what the ingredients of a Chicken Tikka are at the local Indian restaurant (15 points).

....

Signed: ....

Task 10
Find someone who will sing the second verse of the National Anthem to you and get them to sign here (10 points).

....

Task 11
Obtain the signature of the receptionist at Holy Cross Hospital (10 points).

Signed: ....

Task 12
Obtain a cup of spring water (5 points).

Task 13
After 55 minutes return to the Church Hall and give the lady there a two-minute talk on what being a Christian means (15 points).

Total points here: ....

TNT scavenger hunt

This works on the same basis as the previous hunt, but this time points are awarded according to the items found by each team. Adapt the list of items to suit your group and area.

TNT Scavenger hunt task sheet

Your team has 30 minutes to score the maximum points by finding as many of the following items as possible:

a Coca-Cola can (5 points)
a 1980 2p piece (10 points)
a snail shell (5 points) with the snail in it (20 points)
a paper-clip (2 points)
a pine needle (2 points)
a fungus (5 points per centimetre of diameter)
a rubber band (5 points)
a red leaf (10 points)
a piece of green grass (1 point)
a piece of chewed gum (7 points)
a used bus or train ticket (4 points)
a used stamp (3 points)
a live frog (100 points)
a straw (4 points)
an ice-lolly stick (2 points)
an acorn (6 points)
a feather (11 points)
a clothes peg (6 points)
a live fish (16 points)
a button (2 points)
a golf tee (12 points)
a road cone (10 points)
a copy of the local paper (6 points)
a 4-inch twig (5 points)
a piece of wire (8 points)

Survival scavenger hunt

Aim

To encourage teamwork and to have an excellent time!

Equipment

Location: we used a local beauty spot but it could just as easily be played in any location from town to country with appropriate clues.

Ribbons or wool of different colours, two Clue Sheets per team (see below), one Survival Sheet per team (see below), and transport if you are doing the hunt some distance from your usual meeting-place.

Preparation

If your group is in need of a more demanding type of scavenge, if they have lots of energy to burn off and an eye for a challenge, then this one is for you. This is a hunt in which each team's ability to solve clues and then act on them will determine whether they "survive" the game.

You will need to visit your chosen location just before the hunt to arrange the ribbons and the clues.

The pieces of ribbon or wool are colour-coded as follows:

red = fire/warmth
blue = water
yellow = shelter
green = food

Lay the ribbons out in the same order as the clues, so that one clue follows on from another. Even if the groups do not manage to solve one of the clues, they may still look in the area for their supplies.

Here are some sample clues. Write clues of your own which will be appropriate to your group and your locality.

Ye olde survival clues

1. In the valley beneath log bridges
   Lies the hidden fire.
2. Across the bog of eternal stench
   The ribbon lies, your thirst to quench.
3. Skeleton branch over oozing swamp,
   Refreshment may be found.
4. Where the water meets the reeds
   Overhangs a branch with seeds.
5. If you want a tasty dish,
   Try a platform where they fish.
6. Hidden in yellow fungus bunch,
   Something good for you to munch.
7. Where the water leaves the lake
   Another water source to take.
   You might also want to hide chocolate bars or sweets for the
teams to find.

Action

Each team must find so many ribbons to survive and must find
as many as they can before the other teams do. Required
supplies for survival:

Survival sheet

1 fire ribbon per team
1 water ribbon per person
1 shelter ribbon per team
1 food ribbon per person

Give the teams a stipulated time to complete the hunt and let
them go.

Hint

This activity may also be used as a discussion-prompter for another week's session. The young people can discuss how they felt when they could not find the supplies they needed to survive. This could lead into a discussion about hunger and poverty.

BIKE RODEO

Equipment

Cones, a stopwatch, tall canes, string pegs. Some of the members will need to bring and share their bikes.

Preparation

Choose the games to play. Make sure that the playing field is available on the evening, and notify the young people well in advance.

Action

When you get to the field divide the group up into two or more teams, depending on the numbers. Everyone has to take part in at least one of the activities. Keep a careful note of the scores, giving the teams regular updates. Award, say, ten points to the team which wins an event, five points to the runners up, and so on.

Any of the following games are usable, but think up others that suit your group and its interests.

Slalam race relay

Lay out a row of spaced cones per team from the start/finish line, making sure there is plenty of space between the rows and about three metres between the cones in the rows.

On the command "Go!" the first person from each team gets on the bike, weaves through the cones to the end of the row and then back again. When he/she is over the line the next person mounts up and does the same. The first team to complete the course is the winner.

Sudden death sprints

Two riders from each team (three if there are only two teams) line up at the start. On the whistle, they have to cycle to the finish line 50 metres away. The last one over is eliminated and scores one point. They then turn round and sprint back: the last one this time is eliminated and scores two points. Continue until there is only one rider left, and he scores two more points than the rider he eliminated. Add up the team points, and the one with the most wins.

No hands trial

Each team chooses a champion to cycle the 50-metre distance without using his/her hands. The contestants go one at a time and cannot touch the handlebars with their hands after they have crossed the start line. The winner is the rider who gets to the finishing line in the shortest time, or the one who gets nearest to the line.

Bike hurdles

Lay out a series of hurdles made from the canes, the string and the garden pegs. The string needs to be below handle-bar height. One player from each team has to go at a time, riding up to the hurdles, dismounting, going under the string, re-mounting etc. When they reach the end of the course they mount up and cycle straight back. The fastest team wins.

Balloon mace massacre

Set up the canes in a row at the end of the 50 metre course. Tie an inflated balloon to the top of each one. If you have enough canes for each team to have five, then you can play all at once. If not, they will need to take it in turns. The first players are armed with a tightly rolled sheet of newspaper. They bike down the course, hit a balloon with their clubs until it bursts, cycle back and give the bike and club to player number two, who does the same to the second balloon. The first team to wipe out their balloons are the winners.

Ball in bucket

Set up one bucket per team at the far end of the course and a pile of tennis, airflow etc. balls with each team. The first player rides down the course and drops the ball in the bucket without touching the ground and rides back. As soon as he/she is over the line the next player can go. The team that gets the most balls in the time is the winner. Any balls that bounce out or any scored where the player touches the ground don't count.

At the end of all the games count up the scores and announce the winning team, then return to base for refreshments.

IT'S A KNOCKOUT

This is always a popular activity with this age, especially if it involves water and mess. It's a Knockout is great for mixing with other youth groups. Challenge two or three local groups, and each group has to bring a set number of teams and games. Devise games to suit the equipment you have and what your young people are in to. Here are some games for a start:

Blindfold course

Equipment

Chairs, tables, a rope, a paddling pool, string, tyres and anything else!

Preparation

Lay out an obstacle course with whatever is available. Competitors have to climb over, through, round and under it.

Action

One person from each team is blindfolded and has to get from one end of the course to the other. Team members yell helpful advice while the opposition try and send them the wrong way. Have a couple of spotters to prevent them coming to any harm. Let a player from every team have a go. The fastest time wins. This game is good for stimulating discussion about faith and trust.

Tyre race

Equipment

One very large inner tube per team.

Preparation

Mark out the start and finish lines.

Action

Each team has to roll four of its members up the course. They have to lie round the inside curve of the tube and they must not touch the ground. One person is in the tyre, while the rest roll the tyre. When a person is deposited at the far end of the course they remain there while the rest roll the tyre back and choose which member to transport next. The game gets harder after each round. The winners are the first team to get four players rolled over the finish line.

Wet wellies

Equipment

Two large containers (water barrels are ideal), one of them full of water, two very large wellington boots, string and pegs.

Preparation

Set out start and finish lines ten metres apart and position one barrel at each end.

How to play

1. The game lasts three minutes. The winning team is the one that transports the most water.
2. All the players have to participate in rotation.
3. Player one fills one of the wellington boots with water and then puts it on. He/she runs down the course and empties it in to the empty barrel. Then he/she runs back and tags number two, who has already put on the second boot, and so on.

4. At the end of the three minutes measure the depth of water to find out which team has the most.

Box towers

One team has a supply of cardboard boxes, while the other team are positioned five metres away behind a line with a water butt and a heap of sponges. The first team has three minutes to build a tower, while the other team have to knock it down with the sponges. After three minutes measure the height of the tower and then swap over.

Relay madness

Members of each team run down a course and back, performing a series of tasks. The first team to have all its members finish is the winner. The tasks could include:

* Remove a ball from a pool of water, then a sweet from a plate of flour.
* Run ten times round a hockey stick with your forehead on the handle, and do five press-ups over a plate of custard pie mix.
* Walk across a beam set over a paddling pool.

TEAM CHALLENGES

Team building is an important part of youth work. Challenges are one way of giving young people an opportunity to solve problems as a team. They will have a great time, and their leadership skills will be developed too.

Egg launch

Equipment

Ten garden canes, a funnel, string, two eggs and any other bits that might be helpful.

Preparation

Collect the equipment and write out an Instruction Card.

Action

Give each team a copy of the Instruction Card below. It is best to play this game outside.

Instruction Card

1. Your team's task is to produce an egg launcher using as much of the equipment as you wish.
2. Your team has 30 minutes in which to build its launch mechanism, after which the leaders will bring you a real egg to launch. The one with the equipment is your practice egg.
3. The launcher must be self-standing, i.e. it cannot be stuck in the ground or held by the team in any way.
4. The launch of the egg cannot involve any input of energy from the person launching. You can release something, but you can't push or pull something.
5. When the egg is launched, the distance measured is from the front of the machine to where the egg lands.
6. The team firing an egg the longest distance wins.

Hints

The eggs will travel a wide range of distances, one group of thirteen-year-olds managed twelve metres, so don't fire towards your car or church!

Electric fence

Equipment

A length of rope tied between two trees or similarly stable supports at a height of between 140cm and 150cm, depending on the age and size of the young people.

Preparation

Write out the Instruction Card for the game:

Electric fence Instruction Card

1. The task for the teams is to get all the members over this electric fence in the time allowed.
2. The rope, what it is connected to and the invisible curtain underneath it are all super-charged with electricity. Should you touch them or try to go under the rope you are dead for four minutes and cannot talk or help during that time.

Action

Because there is a risk element in this game you will need an adult spotter to ensure that no one is hurt.

The spotter can also act as time-keeper and notify dead players when they can re-enter the challenge.

The winning team is the one that gets all its members over in the fastest time, or more usually the team that gets most members over.

Arrows

Equipment

Four A4 sheets of blue paper with a large arrow on each and four red pieces of paper with a large arrow on each.

Preparation

Produce a copy of the Instruction Sheet for each team.

Arrows Instruction Sheet

1. Note the starting position of your arrows. This is where they have to be returned to if you want to start again.

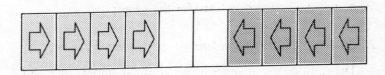

2. The task is to move all the red arrows to the blue end and all the blue arrows to the red end.
3. There are only two possible moves:
(a) an arrow can move one space forward if the space in front is empty;
(b) an arrow can hop forwards over an arrow of the opposite colour.
4. The following moves are not permitted:
(a) to move backwards;
(b) to move into an occupied space;
(c) to hop over more than one opposing arrow at once;
(d) to hop over an arrow of the same colour.
5. The team that can complete the task in the quickest time is the winner.

Action

Note the starting time and make sure that no cheating goes on. If the rules need clarifying, help them out, but otherwise see how long it takes. It could be 30 seconds or 30 minutes!

Blind numbers

Equipment

One blindfold per person, and a large empty space or field.

Preparation

Produce a copy of the Instruction Sheet for each team.

Blind numbers Instruction Sheet

1. Your task will be to line yourselves up in numerical order.
2. You must do this without any form of verbal communication.
3. Every member of the team will be blindfolded and dispersed around the field.
4. Only when the leader has led you away will you be given your number.
5. The numbers will range between one and the number in the team.
6. You will have five minutes of planning time before you are blindfolded and dispersed.
7. The team who do it in the shortest time are the winners.
8. When you think you have lined up in numerical order, call over the leader, who will say yes or no.

Action

1. Disperse the team members around the field, making sure that they are well disorientated. Let them know their number, and tell them that they cannot do anything until you yell "Go!"
2. When all the teams are dispersed, yell "Go!" Note the starting time and the time when each team finishes.

Crate crush

Equipment

One milk crate per team.

Preparation

Produce a copy of the Instruction Sheet for each team.

Crate crush Instruction Sheet

1. Your task is to support the whole team off the ground for five seconds.
2. The only equipment you can use is the crate provided.
3. The team that can do the task quickest and safest wins.

Action

Give an Instruction Sheet to each team, and start timing. If they haven't finished within 20 minutes, stop and debrief. Otherwise, debrief when they have finished the task. Talk about the different aspects of teamwork, leadership, communication etc.

BACKWOODS EVENING

Arrange with your local Scout leaders to take the group on a backwoods evening or night. They will have to build shelters, light a fire, cook a meal they have captured/gathered etc. As well as being a highly challenging evening for the young people, it will help the youth group leadership to develop good links with the Scouting movement.

9

Gospel Worksheets

What is the Gospel?
Do the Gospel Rock
Why Share the Gospel?
Communicating the Gospel
Hold Out for the Power!
What Moulds You?

GOSPEL WORKSHEETS

WHAT IS THE GOSPEL?

MARK 1:1A "THIS IS THE GOOD NEWS ABOUT JESUS CHRIST THE SON OF GOD"

① WARM UP → IN THIS SPACE →
WRITE WHAT YOU THINK THE GOOD NEWS IS:

PAUSE HERE

YOURS
[ ]

② GET TOGETHER WITH THE REST OF YOUR TEAM — SHARE YOUR ANSWERS. DISCUSS, AS A GROUP, WHAT THE GOOD NEWS IS AND THEN WRITE IT HERE →

TEAM
[ ]

③ REPORT BACK

④ DE-CODE WHAT PAUL SAYS:

"□◁▷ □◁▷ ⊐□⬚▷ □□<⌐⌐ ▷□ ▷⌐⌐⬚□

⌐⌐⌐ <▷□ ⌐⌐⌐⌐⬚⌐" ⌐□⊐⌐⬚▷

AB	CD	EF
GH	IJ	KL
MN	OP	QR

ST ╳ WX (UV top, YZ bottom)

A = ⌐   B = ⌐

⌐ : ⌐ 6

S = ▷   X = <⸱

⑤ → READ THE FOLLOWING VERSES: →

ACTS 10:34-40
ACTS 13:26-31
ACTS 17:22-31
ACTS 2:22-38

} What do they have in common?

K = _____   2 Thes. 1:5

I = _____   Hebrews 4:15,16

R = _____   Acts 2:24

C = _____   Luke 23:23

D = _____   Revelation 21:4

M = _____   John 12³⁷

H = _____   Matthew 4:23

F = _____   Galatians 5:1

L = _____   John 15:13

E = _____   John 3:16

A = _____   Hebrews 2:17

G = _____   Ephesians 2:8

D = _____   Matthew 6:13

DO THE GOSPEL ROCK

GROOVE TO THAT FOUNDATION SOUND!

(1) READ [TO THE BEAT!] : 1 CORINTHIANS 1:17:26

— SUMMARY —

~ JESUS IS A STUMBLING BLOCK TO JEWS AND YET A FOUNDATION STONE TO US ~

Y R A H N U S

(2) CHANGE 'STUMBLING BLOCK' TO 'FOUNDATION STONE' USING THE CLUES...

1. AT JESUS' CRUCIFIXION THE SKY WENT: _____

2. FAILURE TO DO YOUR BIBLE STUDY IS: _____

3. HELPING TO TIDY CHAIRS AFTER CLUB IS TO _____ THEM.

4. JONAH PROBABLY DID THIS ON THE BEACH.

5. RED NOSE DAY DANCE

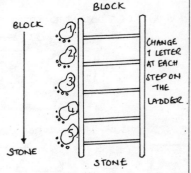

BLOCK

BLOCK

STONE

STONE

CHANGE 1 LETTER AT EACH STEP ON THE LADDER.

(3)

THE MESSAGE OF 'CHRIST CRUCIFIED' CONFUSED BOTH THE JEWS AND THE GREEKS. THE JEWS OFTEN ASKED JESUS TO DO A MIRACLE TO PROVE WHO HE WAS.

JOHN 6:30-35

LUKE 4:22-30

LUKE 11:29-33

JOHN 10:25-33

SPOT THE MIRACLES WHICH WERE MISUNDERSTOOD BY THE JEWS.

ACTION THIS WAY!

THEN READ: JOHN 12:37 → EVEN MIRACLES DID NOT HELP THEM BELIEVE!

(4) THE GREEKS DIDN'T SEE THE SIMPLE MESSAGE OF JESUS. THEY LOOKED FOR SOMETHING COMPLICATED. TURN OVER AND SEE IF YOU CAN CRACK THE CODE TO GET THE VERSE .....!

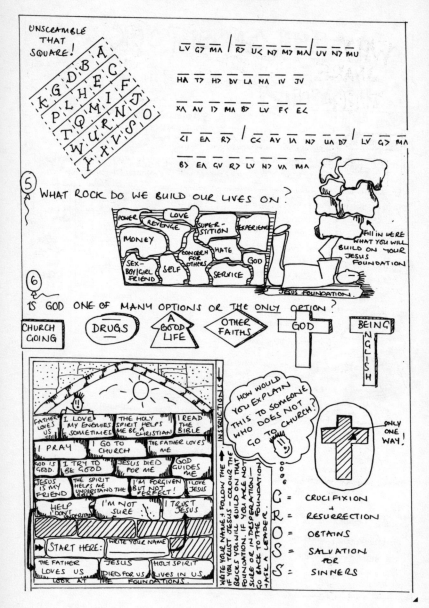

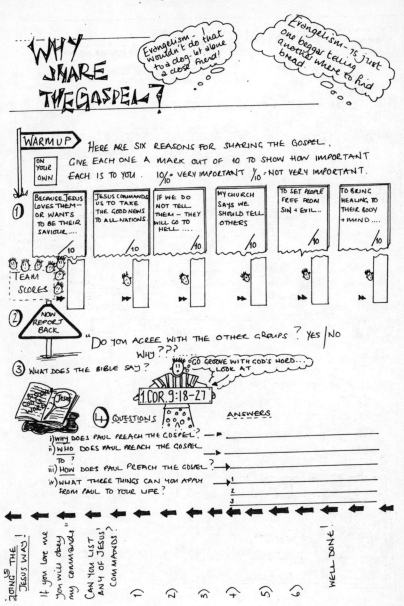

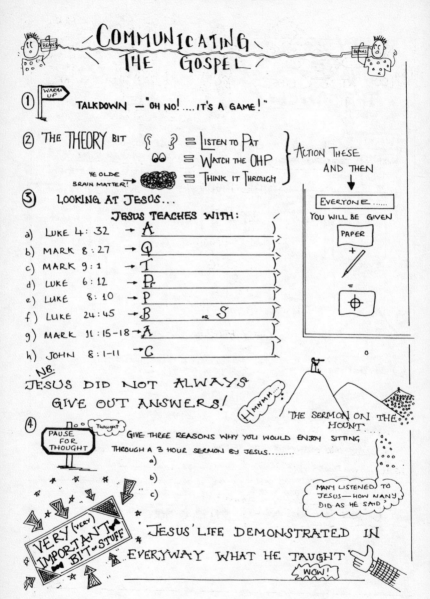

COMMUNICATING THE GOSPEL

① **WARM UP**   TALKDOWN — "OH NO! .... IT'S A GAME!"

② THE **THEORY** BIT   ☰ LISTEN TO PAT   ☰ WATCH THE OHP   ☰ THINK IT THROUGH } ACTION THESE AND THEN

YE OLDE BRAIN MATTER! →

EVERYONE ......
YOU WILL BE GIVEN
PAPER + = ⊕

③ LOOKING AT JESUS...

JESUS TEACHES WITH:

a) LUKE 4 : 32 → A _____)
b) MARK 8 : 27 → Q _____)
c) MARK 9 : 1 → T _____)
d) LUKE 6 : 12 → Pr _____)
e) LUKE 8 : 10 → P _____)
f) LUKE 24 : 45 → B   OR   S _____)
g) MARK 11 : 15-18 → A _____)
h) JOHN 8 : 1-11 → C _____)

NB:
JESUS DID NOT ALWAYS GIVE OUT ANSWERS!

④ **PAUSE FOR THOUGHT**   *Thought*   GIVE THREE REASONS WHY YOU WOULD ENJOY SITTING THROUGH A 3 HOUR SERMON BY JESUS.........
    a)
    b)
    c)

HMMMM

'THE SERMON ON THE MOUNT'

MANY LISTENED TO JESUS — HOW MANY DID AS HE SAID?

VERY (VERY) IMPORTANT BIT of STUFF

"JESUS' LIFE DEMONSTRATED IN EVERYWAY WHAT HE TAUGHT"   WOW!

Now...
PRIVATE
—FOR YOUR EYES ONLY—

⑤ LOOK AT YOUR LIFE..

HINTS BY ERNIE...
AN HONEST LOOK AT OUR LIVES STARTS WITH A LOOK AT JESUS NOT AT OTHERS...

MIRROR, MIRROR ON GOD'S WALL...
WHO'S THE HOLIEST OF THEM ALL?

A

WHAT DOES JESUS SAY ABOUT:

WHAT DO I THINK + DO IN MY LIFE?

SINFUL THOUGHTS

LYING

THE RICH + FAMOUS

SWEARING

CHURCH

HONOURING YOUR PARENTS

UGLY PEOPLE

?

IF YOU ARE HONEST — WHAT JESUS SAYS AND WHAT YOU THINK + DO DON'T ADD UP (GO ON — ADMIT IT!).

IF JESUS HAD ANSWERED THE ABOVE — WHAT HE SAYS AND WHAT HE DOES <u>WOULD</u> BE THE SAME ....

PAUSE FOR PRAYER   "FATHER GOD ... SORRY.."

1992 BAPN

HOLD OUT FOR THE POWER!

1. READ 1 CORINTHIANS 2:4. = WHO IS THE HOLY SPIRIT?

ANSWER: "TRUE" OR "FALSE"

A. THE SPIRIT IS A GHOST, ISN'T IT? ········· (MARK 1:10-12)

B. (ACTS 1:8) ······ IT'S LIKE A FAIRY STORY — IT'S JUST NOT REAL!

C. THE SPIRIT FLOATS AROUND IN HEAVEN ········· (ACTS 5:32)

D. ········· SO THE SPIRIT IS REAL — SO WHAT! (GALATIANS 3:3)

E. ········ WHAT HAS THE SPIRIT GOT TO DO WITH ME — HE'S NOT GOD! (EZEKIEL 36:26-27)

F. THAT SOUNDS FINE — CAN I HAVE IT? ········· (ACTS 8:18-21)

2. WHAT IS THE HOLY SPIRIT LIKE?

A PIECE OF HISTORY....
1 CORINTHIANS WAS WRITTEN BY PAUL IN AD 55 WHILE HE WAS LIVING IN EPHESUS.

IT SHOWS US HOW GOD CAN CHANGE US TO BE MORE LIKE HIM.

READ: 1 CORINTHIANS 2:12
WHAT KIND OF SPIRIT HAVE WE RECEIVED?

CORINTHIANS — HEBREWS — ROMANS — GALATIANS — PHILIPPIANS — COLOSSIANS — THESSALONIANS

PAUL

CORINTH LIBRARY
QUIET PLEASE

JUDGES 6:34

ACTS 2:2-4

JOHN 6:63

GENESIS 1-2

GALATIANS 5:25

2 TIMOTHY 1:7

LUKE 4:18-19

MATTHEW 4:7

P.S
DON'T FORGET TO TUNE IN TO THE NEXT PAGE FOR MORE THRILLS, SPILLS + ADVENTURES AT CORINTH!

TO CORINTH...

FINDING WHAT THE SPIRIT IS LIKE IS LIKE PIECING TOGETHER A JIGSAW. LOOK UP THE VERSES ABOVE AND THE SPIRIT'S CHARACTER WILL COME TO LIFE.

BIBLE INVESTIGATION

▶▶ SPOTLIGHT LUKE 4:18-19.

f - - - - - - | - - ° - | - - - - | - - | - - - |
- - ° .

2. _ r - - - ° - | - - - | - ͤ - - - - - s .

3. _ _ g _ _ | - - - | - - - | - - - - ͩ

4. r _ _ _ _ _ _ | _ _ _ | _ p _ _ _ s _ _ ͩ .

5. f - - - - - - - | - - - | - ₮ - - - | - - | - - - | - - - - 's | f - - - - - - .

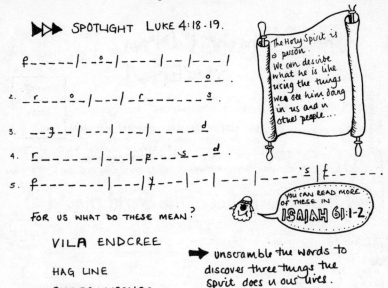
The Holy Spirit is a person. We can describe what he is like using the things wea see him doing in us and in other people...

FOR US WHAT DO THESE MEAN?

🐑 YOU CAN READ MORE OF THESE IN ISAIAH 61:1-2

VILA ENDCREE

HAG LINE

SNIDES + WRONGS

➡️ unscramble the words to discover three things the spirit does in our lives.

▶▶ SPOTLIGHT PAUL.

MISSIONARY JOB-BOOK

CORINTH: POP: 250,000
400,000 slaves
- Big busy trading port
Goods from Spain + Egypt
For the Corinthians the most
important thing is knowledge
(Good library).
Lots of temples.
Goddess Aphrodite is the in-thing
Wicked people.
orgies made o.k. because
Aphrodite is goddess of sex.
- large church needs help...

1. DOES THE DESCRIPTION OF CORINTH SOUND FAMILIAR?
IN WHAT WAYS IS IT SIMILAR TO BRITAIN?

2. WHAT WOULD HAVE BEEN THE MOST EFFECTIVE WAY FOR PAUL TO HAVE SHARED THE GOODNEWS?

3. WHY DID THE PEOPLE RESPOND TO PAUL'S PREACHING?

4. READ 1COR 2:1-5

GOING FURTHER....
"WHAT AREAS OF MY LIFE HAVEN'T I LET THE HOLY SPIRIT INTO?

MEMORY VERSE: 1 CORINTHIANS 2¹² .... WHAT KIND OF SPIRIT HAVE WE RECEIVED?

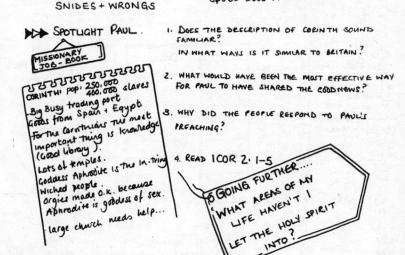

WHAT MOULDS YOU?

1 COR. 15
ROMANS 12 VERSE 2

THE BIBLE TELLS THERE ARE THREE THINGS WE BATTLE AGAINST AS A CHRISTIAN:

1. **THE DEVIL** — A FALLEN ANGEL, WHO WITH ARMIES OF DEMONS ACCUSES AND TEMPTS US.

2. **THE FLESH** — OUR SELFISH DESIRES, THOUGHTS and WANTS. SEX, OUR APPETITES, FOOD, SLEEP, COMPANY, ATTENTION. ETC.

3. **THE WORLD** — THE SINFUL WORLD AROUND US WITH IT'S FALSE TEACHING + PRESSURES TO MOULD US INTO IT'S OWN SHAPE.

1 How Much Does The World mould me? (PUT AN 'X' ON THE LINE)

MOULDS ME A LOT ◄————————————————► DOESN'T MOULD ME

(A) FOR EACH OF THE FOLLOWING GIVE A NUMBER RATING TO SHOW HOW MUCH THEY INFLUENCE YOU IN COLUMN 1.
FOR YOURSELF
1 IF THEY INFLUENCE YOU A LITTLE...
5 IF THEY INFLUENCE YOU A LOT....

(B) PUT THE INFLUENCES INTO PRIORITY ORDER ACCORDING TO HOW MUCH THEY INFLUENCE YOU.
1 = GHEST INFLUENCE
2 = LEAST INFLUENCE
(IN COLUMN 2)

(C) GET INTO GROUP OF 4 AND PUT YOUR GROUP'S TOTALS IN COLUMN 3.

	1.	2.	3.
TELEVISION			
MAGAZINES			
ADVERTISEMENT			
FRIENDS			
FILMS/VIDEOS			
WHAT OTHERS ARE DOING..			
BIBLE			
PARENTS			
YOUTH GROUP/CHURCH			

3 Think About It...

A. WHERE DO WE FIND OUT IF A SONG IS AT NUMBER 1?
B. WHO TELLS US ABOUT THE LATEST FASHION?
C. WHY DO SOME PEOPLE BECOME STARS AND OTHERS NOT?
D. WHAT CAUSES TASTE IN MUSIC/CLOTHES TO CHANGE?

WHO IS RUNNING YOUR LIFE? - ARE YOU...?

REALLY THINK ABOUT THESE QUESTIONS, DON'T JUST BE A **MEDIA CLONE**

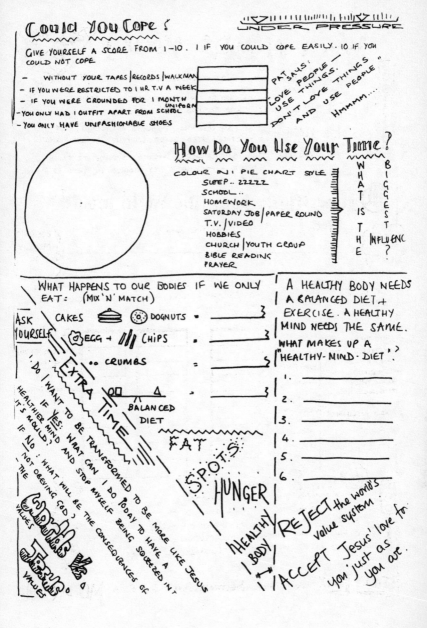

Could You Cope?

UNDER PRESSURE

GIVE YOURSELF A SCORE FROM 1-10. 1 IF YOU COULD COPE EASILY. 10 IF YOU COULD NOT COPE

- WITHOUT YOUR TAPES/RECORDS/WALKMAN
- IF YOU WERE RESTRICTED TO 1 HR T.V A WEEK
- IF YOU WERE GROUNDED FOR 1 MONTH
- YOU ONLY HAD 1 OUTFIT APART FROM SCHOOL UNIFORM
- YOU ONLY HAVE UNFASHIONABLE SHOES

PAT SAYS:
"LOVE PEOPLE / USE THINGS.
DON'T LOVE THINGS" AND USE PEOPLE"
Hmmm...

How Do You Use Your Time?

COLOUR IN: PIE CHART STYLE
SLEEP .. ZZZZZ
SCHOOL ..
HOMEWORK
SATURDAY JOB / PAPER ROUND
T.V. / VIDEO
HOBBIES
CHURCH / YOUTH GROUP
BIBLE READING
PRAYER

WHAT IS THE BIGGEST INFLUENC?

WHAT HAPPENS TO OUR BODIES IF WE ONLY EAT: (MIX 'N' MATCH)

ASK YOURSELF

CAKES — DOGNUTS •
EGG + CHIPS •
CRUMBS =
— BALANCED DIET

EXTRA TIME

FAT
SPOTS
HUNGER
HEALTHY BODY

"... Do I WANT TO BE TRANSFORMED TO BE MORE LIKE JESUS
IF YES: WHAT CAN I DO TODAY TO HAVE A HEALTHIER MIND AND STOP MYSELF BEING SQUEEZED INT IT'S MOULD?
IF NO: WHAT WILL BE THE CONSEQUENCES OF NOT OBEYING GOD?
THE ... VALUES

A HEALTHY BODY NEEDS A BALANCED DIET + EXERCISE. A HEALTHY MIND NEEDS THE SAME.

WHAT MAKES UP A "HEALTHY-MIND-DIET"?

1. _____
2. _____
3. _____
4. _____
5. _____
6. _____

REJECT the world's value system
ACCEPT Jesus' love for you just as you are.

10

Fun Bible Quizzes

The Desert Island
Biblical Connect Four
Biblical Scavenger Hunt
Bible Alphabets
TV Bible Quiz

~FUN~ BIBLE QUIZZES

By painting their King James Bibles blue, St Mary's hoped to reach the youth.

Although Christianity is about a relationship with God through Jesus, and not about learning facts, it can be a useful exercise to test the young people's biblical knowledge. Quizzes can be a fun way to do this. The young people will enjoy the competitive element, and you will be able to discover the areas that need more work and also the individuals who need encouragement. Always bear in mind that the young person who is a convert to Christianity out of a non-church background may be at a disadvantage next to the child of church parents, who has been through Sunday School etc. Also it is good to remember that a church background is not always a sign of conversion!

The desert island

On an A1-size piece of paper draw a map of a desert island with a square grid marked on it. The squares on the grid should be coloured to indicate the terrain, e.g. marsh, forest, sand, grass, cliffs, sea etc. The coves, mountains, hills etc. need to be given appropriate pirate-sounding names. Draw the map so that the easier terrain is mostly round the edges and the worse terrain in the centre of the island. In the centre of the island put an "X" to mark the spot where the treasure lies.

The map needs to be attached to a board so it can be held vertically, and the board needs to be able to take mapping pins with the different pirate teams' flags on them. These will be used as an indication of how each team is doing in the game.

How to play

Divide the group into teams of four. Each team is a group of pirates trying to retrieve the buried treasure that is in the centre of the island.

Team instructions

You will be landing from your boat at one of the sandy bays around the coast. In order for your group to move into any of the squares adjoining the spot where you land, you will need to answer a question of that type. [Either arrange easy questions for easy terrain and difficult ones for difficult terrain, or relate the questions by subject, e.g. grass = Jesus' teaching, mountains = Old Testament prophets etc.]

To answer a question one member of the team comes to the Question Desk and asks for the question relating to the piece of terrain that they want to move into, and then he/she returns to his/her team. When the team knows the answer, the question is returned with the written answer to the Answer Desk. If their answer is correct, the person on the Answer Desk moves the appropriate flag into the square. If it is incorrect, the flag does not move.

Rules

1. Only one player from each team may be out of their seat at any one time.
2. When waiting to collect a question or hand in an answer, pirates must queue up in an orderly manner.
3. There must be no yelling out of questions on the way back to the team from the Question Desk.
4. All answers must be written by a different member of the team, i.e. not the member who collected the question or the one who will return the answer on any one go.

5. No two teams of pirates may occupy the same square on the map at any one time.

6. The winners are the first team to retrieve the treasure, i.e. to gain land on the treasure square and answer a question correctly.

Hints

The coves and terrain must be drawn to make the routes to the treasure equitable.

You will need to write out the question cards: with a Bible dictionary plus your knowledge of what material your group has covered, it need not take long. Keep the map, as you will be able to use it again.

Number quiz

a	+	b	÷	c
−	■	+	■	÷
d	÷	e	+	f
+	■	+	■	+
g	÷	h	+	i

The Bible is full of numbers, so why not use this quiz as a warm-up at the start of an evening to get the young people's brains working and to get them thumbing through their Bibles to check out the answers.

Questions

1. The number of years that Israel ate the manna in the wilderness (Exodus 16:35).
2. The number of years that Jehoram reigned (2 Kings 8:17).
3. Lazarus was in the tomb this number of days before Jesus raised him from the dead (John 11:39).
4. Jesus' age when He started His ministry (Luke 3:23).
5. The number of Noah's sons (Genesis 6:10).
6. The number of thieves crucified with Jesus (Matthew 27:38).
7. The number of olive trees in Zechariah 4:3.
8. How many are good? (Matthew 19:17).
9. The number of years that Abraham dwelt in Canaan (Genesis 16:3).

Biblical connect four

Equipment

A chess/draughts board with counters, or an overhead projector acetate sheet and pens, or a sheet of paper and pens.

Preparation

Write out a list of questions.

How to play

Two teams compete against each other. They are asked questions alternately. If a question is answered correctly, the team may put one of its counters on the board. If a question is answered incorrectly, it is passed across to the other team. The first team to have a row of four counters either on a straight or on a diagonal is the winner.

If your youth group is bigger than eight, why not have a league or knockout competition with matches consisting of three games?

Biblical scavenger hunt

Preparation

Produce one copy of the sheet below for each member of the group.

Passage	Item	Found
1. Ruth 4:7	....	....
2. 2 Kings 3:11	....	....
3. Psalm 45:1	....	....
4. Judges 8:24	....	....
5. Rev. 20:12	....	....
6. Ruth 2:14	....	....
7. Ruth 2:14	....	....
8. Isaiah 65:3	....	....
9. Psalm 68:2	....	....
10. Matthew 13:4	....	....
11. 2 John 12	....	....

12. 2 John 12 ....

13. Acts 4:37 ....

14. Isaiah 62:10 ....

15. Genesis 22:10 ....

16. Ezekiel 5:1 ....

17. Numbers 7:26 ....

Action

Give everyone a copy of the above sheet. Working in pairs, they score one point for every item they correctly identify from the Bible verse and another point for every item they manage to collect within a specified area (either from the local area or from inside and outside your building). Give the pairs half an hour to complete as many questions as possible. The pair with the most points is the winner.

Answers

I have taken my Bible references from the New International Version. They may be different in other translations.

1. Ruth 4:7 = shoes
2. 2 Kings 3:11 = water
3. Psalm 45:1 = pen
4. Judges 8:24 = ear-rings
5. Revelation 20:12 = book
6. Ruth 2:14 = bread
7. Ruth 2:14 = vinegar
8. Isaiah 65:3 = brick
9. Psalm 68:2 = wax
10. Matthew 13:4 = seeds
11. 2 John 12 = paper

12. 2 John 12 = ink
13. Acts 4:37 = money
14. Isaiah 62:10 = stones
15. Genesis 22:10 = knife
16. Ezekiel 5:1 = hair
17. Numbers 7:26 = dish

Ensure that all the items are returned to their rightful places after the game is over.

Bible alphabets

Equipment

A sheet of paper labelled A–Z down the left-hand side, a Bible and a pencil (per person).

How to play

Everyone has ten minutes to try and find a person or a place beginning with each letter of the alphabet. The first one to finish is the winner.

Variations

1. See who can find the most names beginning with a letter in a set time.
2. Limit the challenge to Old Testament or New Testament places or names.
3. Points are scored only for names you get that no one else does.

TV Bible quiz

A good way of doing a Bible quiz is to hold it in the format of a TV quiz show. *Blockbusters* is probably the most commonly used show with this age group, but why not try a *Fifteen to One*-style quiz, where players lose a life when they answer a question wrongly? When a player has lost three lives, he/she is out. The last person who answered a question correctly chooses who is to be asked a question next.

When the number of players is down to three, the game moves into a new phase, where the players can choose either to take a question or to nominate one of the other two to answer. (They must decide before the question is read out.)

The winner is the one who has scored the most points on this final section, or the one who survives the longest. It's easy – record or watch the programme.

Another good programme to take off is *Mastermind*. Have volunteer contestants answering one round of Bible questions and one round of general knowledge questions.

TV programmes change frequently, so choose something which is current and which the young people think is fun, and adapt it for your use.